# ANXIETY

## By

# Danny

ISBN: 9798616968050

First published in UK in 2019 by Karl Wiggins

This edition published in 2020 by Bronwyn Editions

A CIP catalogue record for this book will be available
from the British Library

Typeset by Bronwyn Editions, Berkshire, UK

Printed in Great Britain by Amazon KDP

This book is dedicated to a special human being. A Jack the Lad and a rascal, but kind, funny, loving and thoughtful. Loved by many: Chalkie

# Contents

1.   Anxiety is all in my head
2.   What's it like?
3.   Face the Past
4.   A Gypsy Lad Called Danny (by Karl)
5.   Gypsy Blood
6.   Trouble with a Smile
7.   For My Family
8.   My Gypsy Mum
9.   The Gypsies (by Karl)
10.   Slaves of Pain 1862
11.   The Gypsy Soul (by Karl)
12.   To Clarify (by Karl)
13.   I Am English
14.   God Went to Church
15.   I'm currently in shock.
16.   Holding your Child's Hand
17.   Peter Pan
18.   Let me see you flyTurning Sixty
19.   Sixty Years
20.   My Door is No More
21.   Thoughts
22.   A note from Karl – The Reunion & Danny's Birthday
23.   Further note from Karl - We didn't shake hands
24.   Arribada by Karl Wiggins
25.   Murder
26.   Grief
27.   A note from Karl
28.   Dental Costs
29.   I Turned into a Lunatic
30.   Can you Really Lose Your Mind? (by Karl)
31.   In Fact, I'm not Finished Yet (by Karl)
32.   Harpie
33.   23rd January 2005 by Harpie;
34.   5th July 2005 by Harpie;
35.   Later on, same night, same morning;

36.     29th September 2005 by Harpie;
37.     The First Cut is the Deepest by Danny
38.     DJ Danny
39.     Mental Illness
40.     Alzheimer's took her Mind
41.     Just for the Crack
42.     Bittersweet Morning
43.     We Age to the Grave
44.     Lipstick Lil
45.     My son has flown the nest.
46.     A note from Karl
47.     Hold time in the palm of your hand
48.     Trying to get Answers
49.     When Anxiety Attacks
50.     After Seeking Medical Advice
51.     We are all just Pictures
52.     Half Empty or Half Full
53.     And Laughter
54.     I slept with Miss Anxiety
55.     Skin Cancer
56.     Drink Found Me
57.     Why did Danny write that poem (by Karl)
58.     Time to Go
59.     Kiss Me Goodbye
60.     Miss You, My Wonderful Friend
61.     My old home gone
62.     I Stand
63.     Leaving the UK after the Funeral
64.     Back to the Grindstone
65.     Solitude in my Brain
66.     Cry into the Moon
67.     Peter Pan Will Eventually Die
68.     Children Grown and Gone
69.     We Are All Time Bombs
70.     He Froze in Birmingham
71.     Christmas in a Homeless Heart
72.     Christmas 2018
73.     Another Christmas under Santa's Belt
74.     New Year 2018/2019 (by Karl)
75.     New Year 2018/2019 by Danny

76.   How can I Trust the Doctor?
77.   Just when you think you're all good and healthy
78.   Words to Ease Grief
79.   Old Man Stan
80.   Puzzled Mind
81.   The Only Sane Moments (by Karl)
82.   Let the Music Play
83.   Take one day at a time
84.   Shaking Hands with Tomorrow
85.   Be careful what you wish for
86.   Dementia
87.   Love Lies Bleeding
88.   More or Less Touched (by Karl)
89.   Robin Williams
90.   Having a rough day? (by Karl)
91.   Depression (by Karl)
92.   Anxiety
93.   Keep Busy
94.   Anxiety (by Karl)
95.   Jet (by Karl)
96.   Leather (by Karl)
97.   White Coat Dealer or Doctor
98.   Part Two of White Coat Dealer (by Karl)
99.   Gerbil on the Wheel
100.  Health & Wealth
101.  Along came the Cell Phone
102.  My Wife is a Party Girl
103.  Note from Karl
104.  One Day We'll all be Photographs
105.  An Old Man and His Book
106.  The Bench
107.  Don't Forget to Live
108.  A Soldier's Story
109.  The Gift of Life
110.  Madness into Hell
111.  Forgotten Family
112.  Met Gladys at the Bus Stop
113.  Birthdays
114.  I will never leave you
115.  White Powder Junkie

6

116.  She Kissed me with her Eyes
117.  Nursing Home Alone
118.  I walked a mile with Pleasure (by Robert Browning Hamilton)
119.  Norby – June 8th 2019
120.  The Story of Norby
121.  Inglewood (by Karl)
122.  Norby continued
123.  Norby
124.  Prostate
125.  27 Years
126.  For All Fantastic Dads (on Father's Day)
127.  Goodbye Doesn't Last Forever
128.  Beds are for Flowers
129.  Slave to the Needle
130.  This is What I Have to Deal With (almost all the time)
131.  Life of a Handyman
132.  Neurosis - For those who don't understand
133.  So if I hate labels …..
134.  Anxiety and worry and all that neurotic stuff
135.  George in the Hole (by Karl)
136.  There are no answers
137.  Decisions (by Karl)
138.  I'm on that road to nowhere
139.  Bloody anxiety is running the show
140.  Party for my Brain
141.  A Puppy's Tale
142.  Time to let go
143.  Do it Now
144.  Time we Have
145.  A person can be just sitting there ….
146.  What NOT to say to someone suffering from anxiety
147.  Thoughts of Suicide
148.  He Smiled
149.  No one sees him
150.  Murder
151.  (by Dave the Boxer)
152.  (a note from Karl)
153.  The Sentencing (by Danny)
154.  A note from Karl

155. My letter to the Attorney General's Office (by Karl)
156. Intermittent Explosive Disorder (by Karl)
157. A note by Dave the Boxer
158. Recent Sentences (by Karl)
159. So where did it all go wrong (by Karl)
160. Diminished Responsibility
161. By Danny
162. I have Always Danced
163. Sixty-two
164. Body Parts
165. Anxiety and weak minds
166. Calm those seas
167. Citalo pram
168. Happiness is inside
169. Dirty old man
170. RIP Caroline Flack
171. Thoughts
172. Karl's thoughts
173. Back to Danny's thoughts
174. And after all that
175. A big thank you
176. Strip club (by Danny)
177. Black Jack (by Danny)
178. Gypsy warriors (by Danny)
179. Boxer (by Danny)
180. Grief for my pet (by Danny)
181. Tears of a Clown (by Danny)
182. Masters Voice from the Grave (by Danny)
183. Brunette (by Karl)
184. Huckleberry Blue (by Karl)
185. Conmen of London (by Danny)
186. Paul King (by Danny)
187. Toby and Tony (by Danny)
188. The Dancing Gypsy Boy (by Danny)
189. Paprika (by Karl)
190. Ochre (by Karl)
191. Diamond Diggers of Africa (by Danny)
192. The Miner (by Karl)
193. Is the pain worth it? (by Danny)
194. Puppies are not presents, they're gifts

195.  Women
196.  I get blues (by Danny)
197.  I blew it (by Karl)
198.  How to Really Love a Little Boy (by Karl)
199.  Cuckoo's Nest (by Danny)
200.  Here's to the Crazy Ones (by Karl)
201.  A Final Note from Karl
202.  Chovihani (by Karl)

## Foreword by Karl Wiggins

*This book is a mixture of prose, and quite a bit of poetry as my mate, Danny, tries to come to terms with a debilitating mental illness.*

*We start as Danny takes stock of his life and those around him. He is an enlightened and charismatic poet, and he first of all shares several poems on his upbringing and his Gypsy family. Soon, though, Danny begins to notice loss, although he never phrases it quite like that. But we see loss as children fly the nest, loss of his youthful good looks and energy, a possible loss of income and finally the loss of a friend of ours who was savagely murdered by a madman.*

*We won't be mentioning his real name in this book, only his nickname, but he was a great friend to Danny, myself and others, and when he was brutally murdered it sent Danny into dark places in his psyche that he had trouble escaping from. Danny was very much aware that he was in danger of turning corners in his mind and finding himself in even darker places, but being mindful of such was very little help.*

*Sometimes, the only way out of those black and murky passages, where who knows what horrors may be awaiting us as the mind zig-zags around, is to perform your daily routines systematically as they should be, for everyone has the right to be insane, but very few have the right to live there, for who really knows how much fear and revulsion the human mind can endure, yet still cultivate a wakeful soundness of judgment?*

*Many people hold down responsible positions but are really quite mad.*

*So if you find yourself wandering through those dark passages where dreams speak to you and demons taunt you, just remember that the darkness is afraid of you, not the other way around. And follow your daily routine; shave, shit, wash your hands, wash your face etc. exactly as you've always done, for this confuses the darkness*

*"That's impossible," says Alice*

*"Only if you believe it," advises the Mad Hatter.*

*The darkness that sometimes besieges us cannot harm us. It's the darkness in our soul that we should dread.*
*Even during those times when life seems at its darkest, your mind is dazzling and shining and brimming over with thoughts cropping up again and again, bumping into each other, haunting you and leaving no stone unturned. Thoughts with places to go and thoughts with no place to go. Thoughts with intention and thoughts with no intention. Thoughts trying to repress time and thoughts trying to age it onward. Thoughts with ambition and perception and*

no time for drama. Thoughts that focus on living a positive and confident life.

Mostly through his compelling and page-turning poetry, but also through the written word, this book follows Danny's journey as he slips deeper and deeper into mental illness yet fights to offer advice to others with this condition.

You may think, as I do, that a lot of what went on in Danny's mind was due to depression when a young Gypsy boy from Staines, UK, with curly black hair and the swarthy complexion of his race, working the deckchairs on the beach in Bournemouth, chatting up the girls and always being the one to make people laugh, turned around and found he'd hit 60. How did that happen? He flew over to the UK from California, where he now lives, for a big reunion party – which he DJ'd – for those of us who lived and loved in Bournemouth in the late seventies and early eighties, and although some of us hadn't seen each other for 35 years or so it was as if we hadn't skipped a beat. Why is that? Because we're the mischief makers, the misfits, the bohemians, the court jesters, the clowns and entertainers, the eccentric wackos, the carefree scamps, the migrants and vagabonds, and the free spirits. Without people like us the world would be full of humans who are little more than androids. Every last one of us has a spark of mischief in our eyes, and that spark of mischief is what unites us. Which is why some of us who missed each other first time around still feel that connection. Isn't that weird? How can that be? Because we were born with a rainbow in our pockets, simple as that. Not everybody has this. But fortunately, we do.

*So, what happened to that 18-year-old Gypsy boy who had the world at his feet and who had a different girl every night? He suddenly turned 60, that's what. From 18-60 in what felt like 10 years. And that's the start, I think, of Danny's depression.*

*But he terms it Anxiety, and there's no doubt that Danny is 'anxious' now about a lot of things. Losing his friend to murder a year after his 60th birthday and our reunion party, just tipped him over the edge.*

*The problem with being the class clown is not that everybody expects it from you all the time, because they don't, the problem is that the class clown 'thinks' everyone expects it of them all the time.*

*This book, in verse and magnificent poetry is Danny's story as he begins to notice the world around him start to shatter. Yet through all that he offers encouragement and inspiration to those millions of others who also experience anxiety and panic.*

*And hidden between the lines, there is insight and wisdom and magic that can have only come from the Chovihani*

*The wishbone, as they say, doesn't always have to be out of reach, for the Chovihani lives within you, in the cherished and hallowed temple of your soul. You have always had the Chovihani within yourself*

*Karl Wiggins*

# 1. Anxiety is all in my head

The next time I hear someone say that, I'm going to fucking scream. Of course, it's all in the head, but it doesn't diminish the feeling.

I just got off the phone with a family member and to hear the voice of fear is heart-breaking. Anxiety can buckle your knees and freeze you into a helpless situation, but how do you get it? Great question. Can anyone get it? Can people with money, who have no health problems get it? ANYONE can acquire anxiety which, by the way, also comes with depression. There are many ways anxiety comes into your world, it's very common. It's a condition of the brain that has suddenly awoken with fear.

That's right, fear of nothing and everything. From getting old to getting sick to paying bills. Some studies show that it can often come from the family. But why wasn't I worried before? Because I never had a trigger that was pulled in my brain before, that's why.

A while ago I had a stent in my heart. That's like a small tube that keeps the arteries open and helps supply much-needed blood to the heart. They put it in because of the risk of arterial blockage and heart attack. It's pretty horrible when you think about it, but it's an indispensable and lifesaving surgical procedure. The doctor said, "Listen to your body. If anything starts feeling strange or you get pain in the chest or arm etc. get straight to the emergency room."

THAT'S THE SEED, you see. So if you get indigestion, you think it's a heart attack. This, my friends, is the circle of anxiety. In and out of the emergency room, then the night sweats come, then panic, then the hospital again, then once again you're on the treadmill of worry.

Next thing, you're on anti-anxiety tablets which studies show seem to work. If you've never had this condition, you are only one of the few.

Work is stressful, but that's a different stress. The ones that you get treated for are debilitating and, trust me, once the real anxiety and stress kicks in you will understand the condition. You'd better believe that!

So my relative back in the UK has joined the anxiety club and he's really struggling to come to terms with FEAR. He's perfectly normal, but it all started because he also had a stent in his heart …. and the seed was sewn. Panic, psychic tension, depression, fear, sadness, worry, fear of losing your mind, am I going mad? ALL NORMAL THOUGHTS! It's the brain firing on all cylinders but they're all out of whack. You know you're okay, but the feeling just creeps in. Trust me, you're not alone, and as soon as you tell your doctor he's already ahead of the game …. tablets tablets tablets! You're pumped with so many chemicals that the brain shuts down and calmness comes in to give you a break. But next day it starts all over again. People tend to hit the bottle. They call that a quick fix and, trust me, that road will bury you.

SO WHATS THE SOLUTION?

1. Number 1, of course, is to see your doctor. Medication can help
2. Talk to your real friends, ones that understand your condition and are willing to chat
3. Don't wear out your welcome, because friends have their own problems too. What I mean about not bothering your friends too much with your issues is that it can get really hard for friends to help if you're non-stop calling. They too can only take so much
4. You must help yourself. The most important friend you have is YOU. You can't change what you can't control
5. Go for a walk
6. Read a book. It helps your mind to drift as you get involved in someone else's story, either real or fiction
7. You too can help by listening to people and helping them
8. It's not always about you. We're all so wrapped up in our own world that we fail to

see others suffering, which is why I called my family member, and he too was in my boat. We both bailed out into the water together

FUCK ANXIETY AND DEPRESSION. They can be beat, but you must have understanding of the condition. It's a mental illness and once you have it labelled you can address it. Please contact me if you're a silent sufferer. It'll help. I'm never ashamed of anything if I can help just one person. Never fear fear. Let fear fear you

Love ya all

Danny

# 2. What's it like?

If you've never suffered from Anxiety you can't really have any idea what it's like. It's like having an endless tear-up with yourself inside your head, and still somehow managing to keep a happy expression on your face. It's like being hushed and silent yet howling inside. It's like giving the answer you think people want to hear instead of how you're really feeling. It's like laughing just to kid on your life isn't entirely fucked up. It's like feeling you lost something, although you don't know what, but then realising you lost yourself.

The only person I ever lost and wanted back was me.

It's like wanting friends but hating socialising. It's like brimming over with fury, despair, anguish and confusion until all those emotions cancel each other out and all you're left with is a void. It's like wishing you could just forget all the worries hidden away in the darkest corners of your mind, making you replay all your concerns over        and        over        and        over andoverandoverandoveragain.

It's like standing on scaffolding when the boards used to overlap, and stepping backwards, and all you fall is an inch, and your stomach lurches …. But it feels like that lurch is forever

It's like your soul is weeping while your eyes are smiling. It's like feeling as if you bother people just by being alive. It's like wishing you'd never existed.

Apart from that, it's a piece of cake.

Actually, it's not a piece of cake at all. You probably guessed I was being facetious. It's total fear that comes with headache, dizzying, blurred vision, sleepless nights, panic and isolation.

Welcome to anxiety!

And there's no snapping out of it. It's like constantly walking in a haze or a bubble and the trick to get rid of it is to be busy; write, walk, jog or listen to music

It's becoming very common, especially in young adults who fear life and that's the word …. Fear.

Fear grabs you by the throat and kills you! If you let it, it beats your heart, it attack's your brain, it stops you going out and then if anxiety and fear invite depression and panic to the party you'd better have the tools to deal with it. Sunny days are shit, the stars in the night sky have lost their romance, and the best part of dinner in a restaurant is paying the bill and going home to the safety of your own   four walls

It alienates you from the outside world

And don't be fooled by smiling faces. Anxiety is a fucking curse! Breathe deep, breathe deep, music, draw, paint, write and teach your brain to be calm. This will stop the adrenaline from overwhelming your system. Coffee, chocolate and alcohol are off the menu. If you have anxiety, you are alone

When you're young, you're busy and the world is at your feet, BUT once you start to get older and see time fly by, the world becomes a nursing home or a hospital. It becomes a graveyard. It closes in and makes you stop in your tracks

Once that seed is sown it festers like a sore and anxiety makes you pick it till it bleeds.

There is no therapist that can give me my mum and dad back or make me young again, and the only thing to look forward to is age and death, and with that comes anxiety and psychic tension.

That's the truth. I defy anyone not to be affected by watching their parents die or the shock of having a best friend murdered. It really makes anxiety come alive!

# PART ONE

An introduction to my life as it was

# 3. Face the Past

Aftershave was all the rage
And life was at our feet
We danced away the hours
Then went for something to eat

We gathered at The Hole in the Wall
Lovers holding hands
Fresh-faced and silly
I was trying to be a man

Giggling girls and makeup
There was always an ugly friend
I ended up with Sally
Hoped the night would never end

In those days of innocence
When life was so brand new
The stupid things we said
And the crazy things kids do

I got a job as a waiter
And I certainly made people wait
I pissed myself laughing
When a sausage rolled off his plate

Then I found my brother
Karl Wiggins to be exact
We bonded like glue
He always had my back

We both got the giggles
Serving guests at the hotel

Karl was on one side
He was serving as well

The menu was chicken
It came with stuffing and sauce
So when I asked a lady, 'Would you like stuffing?'
She only said, "Of course"

Karl got the giggles
Just a little at first
I said to this old man
You've got some stuffing on your shirt

Thought Karl would die that night
As tears rolled down his face
He kept his composure very well
Then fell all over the place

The funniest thing I have ever seen
Was sweat dripping in a man's pie
I have never laughed so much in life
I thought I was going to die

Karl has many more stories
When I slipped upon the floor
The tray of food went everywhere
As I came flying through the door

And yes, I dropped a gammon steak
On a poor man's baldy head
The gravy dripped on down his neck
I thought that I was dead

He came down to breakfast

A blister for all to see
I said, 'I'm really sorry sir'
As I poured him his hot tea

I still laugh to this day
Every story is true
And when we get together
I'll tell many more for you

I look over my shoulder
How time went by so fast
When I see you all again
I'll have to face my past

# 4. A Gypsy Lad Called Danny
## (by Karl)

*There was a Gypsy Lad called Danny*
*Who'd sometimes grab a granny*
*Back in that famous heat wave*
*When he never could behave*
*It was really quite uncanny.*

*On tables he would wait*
*And often he'd get a date*
*But I looked with dread*
*As on a punter's head*
*He dropped a mustard plate.*

*'Oh no,' said Danny, 'Oh no!*
*Your bonce is all aglow*
*I'm afraid I became distracted*
*To your wife I was attracted*
*For her knockers are all on show.*

*'I wasn't paying attention*
*I'm afraid it's a boner contention*
*Your wife's got a pair*
*I tried not to stare*
*But now there's no pretension.'*

*Danny tried to wipe his face*
*Yet wished he could embrace*
*The lady across the table*
*Whose tits were quite unstable*
*And he couldn't keep a straight face.*

*Next day she called for Room Service*
*And Danny, really quite nervous*

*Took her egg on toast*
*And did his uppermost*
*To show her no disservice.*

*'My husband's had to go*
*I'm all alone don't you know?*
*As a waiter you have no style*
*But won't you stay awhile*
*I've something I'd like to show'*

*Well Danny took the hint*
*To her bed he did sprint*
*He'd given her husband mustard*
*To his wife he now offered custard*
*And in her eye he left a glint.*

*BOOM! BOOM*

# 5. Gypsy Blood

My skin is dark as Oakwood
My hair is black as night
My strength that of an old bear
And by God I know I can fight

No man stands my shadow
My wife is by my side
Our children are our future
We have a sense of pride

At night we tell our stories
We gather one and all
Should there be any trouble
We just put out the call

Our blood is thicker than oil
Our hearts are open wide
Our families stand together
We never ever hide

We follow a code of honour
It's written in our blood
When funerals are at our doorstep
We show a sea of love

My tears are now falling
As I wait for Heaven above
For love runs through our veins
And so does Gypsy blood

# 6. Trouble with a Smile

Born under the stars
Life was at our feet
We struggled by
But we made ends meet

Been pushed into corners
Even forced off our site
Backs against the wall
No choice but to fight

Mum worked the fields
Dad collected scrap
We came from a big family
But we had each other's back

No one came between us
We are a special breed
We believe in sharing
And don't believe in greed

The shirt that I wear
It's yours as a gift
And if you're ever down
We're there to give you a lift

We deal with our problems
We take it to the street
We fight toe-to-toe
To see who gets beat

We follow our traditions
We stay within our clan
When we're told we can't do it

We show them that we can

I'm a tinker, I'm a Gypsy
I'm trouble with a smile
I will listen to a reason
But it may take a while

Don't push me with an attitude
Try not to make a scene
Because there are two sides to Gypsy
One called rage, one called mean

I can smile until tomorrow
I can laugh all day long
I can kiss the ground you walk on
Be the words in your song

But heed and take this warning
It should serve you very well
Walk with me to heaven
Or taste the depths of hell

## 7. For My Family

Hung my head for many years
Children called me names
They called me filthy Gypo
As I walked home in the rain.

But as I got older
I stood and faced my foe
Stood in the playground
Went at it toe to toe.

No one will ever shame me

Proud as proud can be
I belong to Gypsy
As they reside in me.

My blood is thicker than mud
As we all sat around the fire
Respect and honour and tradition
As the flames grew higher and higher.

My mother told us stories
How life was very hard
Picking hops in the wet fields
And the rain that never stopped.

Father went out door to door
Trying to make a crust
Always were the warnings
Gypsies you should never trust.

So fighting was our way of life
I still do it to this very day
And if you don't like Gypsies
You best keep out our way.

# 8. My Gypsy Mum

Bitter was the winter night
As mother came through the door
Just as she had done
So many times before.

She went into the kitchen
Made us something to eat
Rested her broken back
As I rubbed her aching feet.

I was only seven
And didn't understand
Father was in the fields
Working on the land.

I waited for the horse's feet
To sound across the lane
Father sat by the fire
Trying to hide his pain.

Late at night
I climbed into my mother's bed
Felt safe and warm
As she stroked my tired head.

Time had taken toll on Mum
Her health was in decline
We had to call the doctor
We were running out of time.

She called me to her beside

And she held my shaking hand
You will always be my baby
Time to be a man.

I must leave you now
As she pulled me to her side
She kissed my tears away
The ones I tried to hide.

The doctor closed her eyes
As he leaned across the bed
I'm sorry son to tell you
But your mother I'm afraid is dead.

I screamed 'I want my mum'
As my father pulled me away
I begged and begged my father
Please let me stay.

Now that I am older
The pain won't go away
Lucky to have my mother
With me every single day

She's always right beside me
She even holds my heart
My dear mother
We shall never be apart.

So wait for me as I for you
Until my day to come
So proud am I to have you
As my Gypsy Mum.

CELIA WINTER ROSE, MY MUM, MISS YOU MUM
AND DAD

# 9. The Gypsies (by Karl)

The Gypsies are believed to have first shown up in England in the 14th or 15th century, and there's no doubt they had a tough time of it. The Egyptians Act (1530) made it illegal for Romani to enter the country and made it compulsory for those already living here to leave within two weeks. And if they didn't, all their property was confiscated, they were imprisoned and deported. In 1554 the act was amended, and if the Romani promised to give up their "naughty, idle and ungodly life and company" and chose to take on a 'settled' way of life then they would no longer be punished. On the other hand, however, if they didn't then they'd face the gallows. In 1564 a new law presented Romani who were born in the UK with the opportunity of becoming British subjects if they integrated into the local community.

They didn't.

The Romani were subjected to constant and endless hatred, prejudice and racism from the authorities and in 1596 106 men and women were sentenced to death at York, just for being Romani. 97 of them could prove that they had been born in England, but 9 of them were executed.

England started deporting Romani people as early as 1544 and those who endured the hardship of being packed like sardines into a small wooden ship (rolling and rocking at the mercy of the sea, and the abhorrent agony and despair of the foul odours, fumes, seasickness, vomiting, headaches, mouth rot, fever, diarrhoea, constipation, abscesses, scurvy, hallucinations, hysteria and madness, all as a result of eating rotten meat, drinking fetid water and being crammed so tightly together, thus spreading disease quickly) ….. those who survived this passage were sold as slaves and unbelievably continued as best they could the expression of the Romani culture. Somehow the social fabric of their lifestyle prevailed.

In the 17th century Oliver Cromwell consigned British Romani to work on the cotton, tobacco and sugar plantations of the American South. There is authenticated documentation of English Gypsies being owned by freed black slaves in Louisiana, Cuba, Barbados and Jamaica.

And not a lot of people know that.

# 10.　　Slaves of Pain 1862

Waves broke at the hearts of many
The hull was filled with pain
Fathers shackled to their brothers
Never to return again

Children torn from mother's breasts
The horror of the screams
Whips and chains replaced the love
And ended all their dreams

Lust for souls to fill the decks
Death would be their friend
Master's rage was well rehearsed
To seek bitter revenge

Late at night the silent cries
These irons cut me so
Many days and many nights
Such a long way to go

My friend, Mufa, was beaten
His back torn to the bone
They hung him from a jib at dawn
All night long he moaned

Then silence from his broken soul
Cut down like a wretch
Thrown overboard to quail his thirst
Let the sharks do the rest

We anchored in an offshore bay
Many left for dead

The stench of death lay on the boards
Makeshifts for their beds

No pity shown or given
A gallows for a fool
Learn or burn to nil thy mouth
Follow the master's rule

I stood to face the devils
A price lay on my head
Sold to the master bastard
He beat me half to death

There were rules I had to follow
Never look the bastard in the eye
I knew if I dare his patience
I would surly die

Master was the crown of shame
My lips that dreaded word
For one mistake would be all it takes
My voice would never be heard

So I worked and picked the cotton
My back broken by the pain
When the sun kissed me in the morning light
It was back to work again

Many years I toiled the fields
The scars have left their mark
Dreaming of my mother
And how we were torn apart

I long for just a warm embrace
Just a moment's kiss
My dear mother
Tis you I dearly miss

Many years have passed me by
My health is in decline
Been beaten to an early grave
My life was never mine

I cried and died today
I was laid in my grave
Freedom came to take me away
No more to be a slave

# 11.    The Gypsy Soul (by Karl)

*The Gypsy soul isn't missing or off-track. It's just a soul that loves motion and discovering the vibration and rhythm of the planet. A Gypsy thinks this whole ball of wax is nothing but an expressive, literary work of nature. The Gypsy understands and appreciates an inbound and infectious kind of independence.*

*With a horse and cart, a ferret, a dog and a gun, who could not be happy?*

*For the Gypsy, it's moments in time that count, not interpretations or rhetorical questions or resolutions or justifications, and not even the journey's end, for the journey never ends. Just moments in time.*

*Gypsies are living poetry, and they are born for disappearing.*

## 12.    To Clarify (by Karl)

*What gives me the right to discuss Gypsies here? Three things; 1) Danny, 2) a Gypsy fighter I know known as Gawjus who says, "You crack on, mate, you write what you like. Anyone's got anything to say about it, they can talk to me, and if you need any help just let me know," and 3) my great-grandmother, Martha Summers, who was born in Notting Dale. Her father (my great-great-grandfather), Benjamin Summers, was a coachbuilder. He built horse-drawn carriages, Gypsy wagons and Romani caravans, or vardos as they are known as.*

*Gypsy Street in Mary Place, Notting Dale, was described by the author George Barrow as "chock full of crazy, battered caravans of all colours … dark men, wild looking women and yellow faced children," and its reported that the Gypsy camp in Latimer Road, Notting Dale, accommodated 40 to 50 families. To some extent they were seasonal as some of them toured with the travelling fairs, or alternatively they would travel the country hop picking, but it wasn't until the late 1800s that they began to leave their caravans and 'settle' in the houses in this "bag, bone & bottle" district of Notting Dale where a local reporter described the children as "looking blue and peaked on the cold morning, but the majority well-fed and clothed though many hatless and girls with frayed skirts. Many children of dark, gypsy type."*

*As soon as the sun went down in the winter months it's reported that this was Carnival Time, when it was "thronged like a fair ... in the side streets were side shows including vendors of patent medicine and itinerant musicians." Dogfights were commonplace, as were early morning bare-knuckle fights, one of which resulted in a local Gypsy being tried for murder.*

*If Martha had Gypsy blood in her, who knows? But this was the atmosphere my great-grandmother was born into. She had eleven brothers and sisters, their birthdates spanning 22 years, seven older siblings and four younger, but even though my own father spent years studying the family tree and, indeed, wrote two books on genealogy, my great-grandfather's lineage remains a mystery. It just stops at his own grandparents (my great-great-great-grandfather). We've never been able to trace the Summers family further back than that. Certainly, as mentioned, Benjamin Summers, who married a girl from Bethnal Green, was a coachbuilder, and he himself had nine brothers and sisters. His father was also a coachbuilder, but all we know about his father was that he was known as William, and his wife was called Ann. And that's it.*

*With eleven brothers and sisters, plus nine uncles and aunts and I can't imagine how many cousins, there's no doubt they would have been a formidable family with close links to the indigenous yet itinerant Gypsy composition of the neighbourhood, even more so through Benjamin's work as a coachbuilder*

*As I say, I'm not convinced that Martha had Gypsy blood in her at all, although I'm told she "had a presence about her" and that she "had the look," in that her eyes would turn fierce and intense when angered. Martha was quite daunting, and she was my great-grandmother.*

*What does it take to call yourself Gypsy? 20 or 30 years on the road? That won't make you a Gypsy. It's a birth right and family bloodline, that's what makes me a Gypsy*

*People whose only claim to fame is that their own parents or grandparents were at Woodstock hardly have a right to call themselves Gypsy. And neither do I. But I do at least have the right to write about them.*

# 13. I Am English

Born of bread and butter
Marmalade and jam
Trifle and custard
Corned beef and ham

Tea and crumpets
Strawberries and cream
Watching tele on Sunday
Life was but a dream

Dad sat by the fire
Mum was in her chair
My sister in the mirror
Playing with her hair

Time flew by so quickly
After man landed on the moon
Top of the Pops on Thursday
Waiting for the tunes

We had Jackanory, and Magic Roundabout
Sooty and Sweep as well
We chased each other around the playground
As the teacher rang her bell

School dinners tasted awful
But got seconds if you wanted more
You always saw the scruffy kid
And knew that he was poor

Left school when I was fifteen
Got a job straight away

But freezing cold on the building site
I knew I wasn't going to stay

Booked a flight to California
Sun, sea and sand
By the time I looked over my shoulder
I'd soon become a man


## 14.    God Went to Church

God sat in the back row
Large doors led him in
Gold encrusted crucifix
A choir singing a hymn

His son was hung on a silver cross
Pearl drops fell like tears
Faithful gathered like moths to a flame
Been doing it for hundreds of years

Column-gilded cherubs
Marble inlaid floors
Pulpit adorned with platinum
Oak hand-crafted doors

A silver plate was passed around
Sinners paid for their past
Water sold in paper cups
Or hell you shall be cast

Gold and silver ceilings
Candles set the scene
Priest covered in a pure white gown
My God, how obscene

God let out a mighty roar
This shall not be in my name
The poor lie sleeping on the streets
You all should be ashamed

You don't need a church to pray
For I am in your heart
You don't need a golden cross
For we shall never part

I'm with you in your darkest hour
No gold could palm my hand
Look deep inside your soul for me
For this is where I am

God was very angry
All that glitters is not gold
Many of my children are hungry
And are living in the cold

God screamed, Remove those crosses
Sell them and feed the poor.
He shook his fist in anger
Then God kicked open the door

God went back to heaven
Said, I gave them free will to live
All I ask is they love each other
And teach them all to give

When you wake up tomorrow
I hope you open your eyes
For many are living in poverty
For them there's no surprise

# 15.    I'm currently in shock.

I am gutted and very, very sad.

I first arrived in California in 1978. It was a wonderful place. It was fabulous to walk down Venice Beach watching the entertainers, and it was great to walk from Santa Monica to Venice with my family and show them where I'd ended up. It was brilliant! Such a vibrant experience!

But fast forward to today, or should I say this morning ... the place is a shithole, a disgusting shithole with homeless camped out all along The Boardwalk. Broken bottles, bikes, shit, cans, it looks like a battle zone. There must be between 500 and 1000 vagrants that have taken over a tropical paradise.

If you're planning on coming over to visit Venice Beach …. Don't. Keep away. I'm so sad to tell you this but it's a really disgusting place. I'm heartbroken to see Venice this way.

And why are all these people homeless? In this day and age, when every home has to have a microwave, air conditioning, satellite TV, a large fully-stocked freezer, and ginger & pink pepper reed diffusers, why do we still have homelessness? And how many of these people fought    for    their    country?

If we can build tent cities to house illegal aliens, why can't we build tent cities to house ex-soldiers who are currently on the streets?

The USA is currently the 13th richest country in the world, meaning that there are 183 countries where the level of wealth, comfort, material goods and necessities available to everyone is not up to the quality of life in the United States. And yet we still have people sleeping in bus stops!

Shame on Los Angeles City.

# 16.  Holding your Child's Hand

Not easy being a parent
In fact, it's hard as hell
You hope you've done a good job
But only time will tell

The worry of tomorrow
Many nights without sleep
You tiptoe in the bedroom
Making a promise you must keep

I promise I'll be there
I'll always be by your side
I'll hold you in my arms
Wipe your tears when you cry

I will be your strength
Just call out my name
No mountain or storm shall stop me
I'll even run through flames

I chased her with a giggle
As sunlight caught her hair
Time ran beside us
Suddenly she wasn't there

I cherished every moment
Alas time has won
But many years later
We were blessed with a beautiful son

The road of life is a mystery
Destiny holds hands with fate
I taught them everything I knew

To love and not to hate

Now I am but an old man
Bittersweet the taste
Every moment captured
Nothing went to waste

Those days I can still remember
Passed by like wind and sand
The sadness that I feel inside
Letting go of my children's hand.

## Buying Time

I met a wise man who never grew old
He told me of his age
He showed me pictures in a book
As he slowly turned the page

'There is a far-off land that time forgot
Its valley fell to the sea
They say time has stopped since time began
But you can buy time from me'

How much for my youth again?
What price will I have to pay?
'Fill my hand with gold or silver
And time won't slip away'

Your prices are very high, my friend
But buying time is my task
I want to be young again
I shall give you what you ask

I filled his hand with treasure
As much as he could hold
No need to wait until tomorrow
For I'm not getting old

We laughed away the hours
As he gave me a wink of his eye
'I have to tell you something
You do know you'll never die

'You shall live for ever
No need to buy a grave

And while your friends pass away
You will always remain

'Time will be your best friend
It will never let you down
It will never run out on you
It will always keep you around'

He tipped his hat and said goodbye
As he wandered down the road
I screamed so loud to wake the dead
I said, Sir, please don't go

I want to change my mind
I want to now grow old
'That will cost you double my friend
So fill my hands with gold'

So once again I filled his palms
With gold and a tear in my eye
The wise man looked at me and said
Don't let time pass you by

# 17.    Peter Pan

Peter Pan had a plan
Never to get old
He never worried about a thing
Said all that glitters is not gold

Take life real easy
Smell flowers every day
Walk and blow a kiss to the sky
Watch your problems go away

Stress will take you to an early grave
Worry will hold your hand
Don't think of the future
It never turns out as you planned

Just live for the moment
And you will always stay young
Laugh and sing as much as you want
And dance into the sun

Let rain wash over you
Let it cleanse your soul
Always look over your shoulder
There's still many miles to go

Tears will stain your pretty face
Heartache will waste your time
Burden will break your back in two
It's time to change your mind

So if you want to be like Peter Pan
Listen to my every word
You can follow a different path

Or stay within the herd

Spread your arms far and wide
Try and touch the sky
And those of you who are young at heart
**Let me see you fly.**

# 18.    Turning Sixty

Only seemed like yesterday
When life was at my feet
Met up with all my mates
And played out in the streets.

Time flew by so quickly
A path led me away
Looking over my shoulder
A boy that didn't stay.

Left home with a vision
An adventure to taste my lips
The world was at my doorstep
Time to take that trip.

A new horizon greeted me
Sand, sea and sky
Let me taste tomorrow
Until the day I die.

Pages turned as pages do
My life is an open book
I left my home as a boy
The chances that I took.

Every year that passes
I leave a part of me
Tuning sixty in a few weeks
I'm happy I'm able to see.

Many friends died early
They never got to age
Their voices still reside in me

It still leaves me with rage.

So sad their innocence taken
Just tears are left behind
The world keeps on turning
We're all running out of time.

So here's to my 60<sup>th</sup> birthday
I'm happy I'm still here
I pray I see sixty-one
I hope to see you all next year

## I'm Like a Car Turning Sixty

Nothing works anymore
If you get my drift
I try to get into second gear
But the bastard won't even shift

A headlight lost a bulb
The window wipers are broke
The oils needs changing
And now I have to pull out the choke

My tires are now balding
The rubber don't touch the road
There are so many miles on the meter
Ain't got too long to go

The paint is cracked and peeling
The engine sounds real bad
The carburettor needs cleaning
Can someone pass me a rag?

I used to be fast as lighting
The engine purred like a cat
I had a cheetah in my tank
Do a hundred miles flat

My seats were soft as velvet
My gear shift made of steel
My driving was fantastic
When I was behind the wheel

I could burn rubber
Go miles on a tank of gas

The power that was in my engine
Could pass you in a flash

But now I'm a collector's model
People pass me by
Lots of people look at me
But no one wants to drive

They put me in a showroom
No one sees my tears
The window wipers finally work
After all these years

I'm waiting for a mechanic
To adjust my brakes and clutch
Just a little oil
Or a gentle loving touch

And now I'm turning sixty
A classic on the track
A tow truck arrived this morning
They're trying to get me back

They put Viagra in my engine
Gave me a lick of paint
Greased up my prop shaft
And put petrol in my tank

I'm ready to turn sixty
And hope I turn a head
Just because I'm sixty
Doesn't mean I'm dead

I'm revving up my engine
I'm letting off the brake
Turning sixty ain't a death sentence
Turning sixty is a piece of cake

# 19.  Sixty Years

If you're lucky
You get to be old
When you're young
You own the world

You dance and sing
And play all day
Then off to school
Then go out to play

There's food in the cupboard
And a roof over your head
And every weekend
You can snuggle up in bed

Mum in the kitchen
Dad's in his shed
He's tinkering around
Not hearing what mum said

We sat around the TV
Dad in his chair
Mum right beside
She was always there

Then eight o'clock
Got told to go to bed
Flashlight under the covers
Reading comics instead

Then time passed
As did Mum and Dad
Gone are the memories

Good times we had

Now I put food in the cupboard
It's me who goes to work
I try to move around
But my bloody back hurts

Lost my hair to history
My six-pack became a keg
Starting to limp a little
When I hurt my leg

My hips have stopped dancing
But I still try to look young
I get called Popsie
From my oldest son

His friends call me sir
That really makes me feel old
Now it's me who goes to be bed
From my son that I'm told

Life and age
Go hand in hand
No one knows
What life has planned

Sixty is sexy
That's what I'm told
I think they're lying
Because I feel very old

# 20.   My Door is No More

Born on a cold winter's day
The snow fell like rain
Sat around the fire
How I'd love to do it again

Those days lost in memory
Some full of regret
Looking over my shoulder
Some I could not forget

Mum's home was her kitchen
Dad's was in the shed
Laughter gone forever
Laughing at the things Mum said

The fields were my playground
The trees I'd love to climb
We would play hide 'n' seek
And always ran out of time

Mum called out the window
Time to have my tea
My hiding place was given away
Hiding up the tree

Innocence and my boyish smile
Those days etched in my mind
My father's arms were always there
My mother's not far behind

Dark days found a silent home
A knock came to our door
I just remember my father's face

As he broke down on the floor

I was only seven years old
When Nan passed away
My poor old dad was heartbroken
I can still see his face today

Then Mum too suffered in silence
Grief came to our life
Time just goes by every day
I could hear her cry at night

Now that I am older
My youth has passed me by
I lay awake in the middle of the night
And just like Mum I cry

Children find their folded wings
It's time to fly the nest
Parents kiss them goodbye
We tried to do our best

I went to take a journey
And make my way back home
To relive my childhood
And see how far I've come

"Where you going mate," said the driver
As I sat in the back all alone
29 St Michael's Road
"Sorry mate, that place is gone"

He took me to a housing estate
Trying to catch my breath
Looking around the houses
Just to see what's left

I stood and cried like a baby
Buckled to the core
Just one wish to be granted
To knock upon my door once more

# 21.    Thoughts

I'd like to say a big thank you to friends who like or dislike my poems. While I know I write like a six-year-old, I'm overwhelmed by your encouragement.

It's always been a passion to write about life; NOT trees and happy shit but depressive and overbearing situations; grief, sadness, doom and gloom, but it's not depressing to write. It's a wonderful feeling to express how someone feels when a pet or a parent dies.

And by no way am I depressed or suicidal. Far from it. We all live in a sad world and I've found a way to express the way I feel. Is this world awful? Yes, it's hard, it's emotional and it's tragic. We are all finding happiness one way or another, but as I've said before, LIFE IS SHIT. It's no bowl of cherries. We have to find a cherry in the shit.

I know the choice of poems and the topics I write about are very dark, but it's my way of dealing with my anxiety, so a big thank you to all who find a cherry in my poems. Seek what light brightens your day for a fleeting moment. A kiss from a heart is passion enough for this world we live in. It really is very tough.

Danny

## 22. A note from Karl – The Reunion & Danny's Birthday

*Six hundred years ago they'd have burned all of us as Witches.*

*Cluttered and sloppy and chaotic, we may be, but we're easy on the eye and we're getting warmer.*

*There are people who'd accuse us of being mentally ill. Bizarre as it may seem, even as recent as the 1950's 'hospitalisation' was a commonplace treatment for 'tormented' youth. Many youngsters who did not acquiesce to the strict and severe social benchmarks of their families were sectioned in these 'hospitals.' Sometimes the most insignificant social violation would be reason enough to send them away.*

*Yes, we're drunken, we're disorderly, we're impulsive and at times we're lawless, but without us, well, wouldn't this planet be a boring place to live?*

*We are the riotous, reckless and rebellious people who from time to time tilt the world on its axis a little bit. The world needs that.*

*Now I'm the philosopher-poet, and I know that means I'm a little bit touched. But as I've said many times before if everyone's going to think of me as nuts then at least it redeems me from being average.*

*So perhaps being a bit whacko isn't so bad. And in my defence – because I am going somewhere with this – I'm not really a lunatic (although I'm sure I've had my moments). All of us, you see, are conscious and alive in a lunatic world, and for that precise reason ordinary people – we can call them Grokels if you like - will call us lunatics.*

*To explain that, I was working a construction job where there were a crowd of quantity surveyors. Now, this isn't to be confused with land survey engineers. This lot's job involves cost planning and cost estimating, procurement and tender advice, asset capitalisation and so forth. They weren't lunatics and they weren't unruly. In fact, they're the type who would often accuse unruly people of being immature.*

*Anyway, we were all in the pub one night, the QSs, me, a bunch of other blokes from site, when one of the QSs said to me, "Do you know, I can honestly say this is the best bunch of mates I've ever had." I was absolutely astounded. You could have knocked me down with a balance sheet. This lot were so humdrum and uninteresting. They dressed the same socially as they did for work; trousers, the same type of characterless shirt, sleeves rolled down to the wrists with the buttons done up tightly, no visible tattoos. You were never going to have a really wild night out* with this lot. They were never going to choose the 'Take the psycho path' at the fork in the road. And you could never count on any of them to back you up in a scrap.

And yet this geezer felt that they were the best bunch of mates he'd ever had!

What happened to the wild years when he was supposed to be carefree? I'll tell you; They skipped him by, that's what.

We had a three-day party in Bournemouth on the weekend of 24th – 26th November 2017. This was a combined reunion for those of us who were in Bournemouth in the late 70s and early 80s and Danny's 60th Birthday. Danny flew over from California and, of course, DJ'd the event.

So indulge me if you will because I know there were people who wanted to come to our '76 reunion party on November 25th 2017. Some had every right to be there. They were part of the Bournemouth / Boscombe scene of the late 70's and early 80's and others who, despite their exaggerated sense of their own importance, are not of our tribe. They either arrived in Bournemouth a decade ago, or they've never even lived in Bournemouth at all, yet still thought they could gate-crash our party.

I repeat, our tribe are those of us who lived and loved and laboured through those hard yet *hysterical years in Bournemouth. For us and our families; our wives and our husbands and our kids, and nobody else.*

*What made that weekend so special? There were people I hadn't seen for over 30 years, and yet it was as if we hadn't seen each other for a month. How can you explain that? Thirty, thirty-five, forty years, there were even people who'd missed each other first time around, yet when we talked it was as if we hadn't skipped a beat. All of us have a very rare and exceptional connection. It's pure magic.*

*And right now, you're probably thinking what's all this got to do with anxiety, depression and mental illness? Well, stay with me, because I'm going somewhere with this;*

*Five o'clock Friday*
*All neat and tidy*
*We entered the hotel reception*
*To meet Steve and Sandy*
*For just a quick shandy*
*Then in walked the rhythm section*

*There was Dave & Lorraine*
*And a bottle of champagne*
*And Danny and Chalky too*
*A Chinese had been booked*
*But we'd overlooked*
*How long since we'd last said adieu*

It was called Gander on the Green
Yet this weird time machine
Messed with my recollection
Now Sir Christopher Creek
Held the mystique
But I certainly knew the direction

While they checked out the venue
We examined the menu
And nibbles arrived from the bar
Faces I hadn't seen in thirty years
Were walking in full of cheer
It was surely the best night so far

First Tony Caves
From the California waves
I hadn't seen Tony in a while
Then Erica and Geordie Trish
Both looking a dish
Arrived at our table with a smile

It was so surreal
You can see the appeal
Of old friends reunited
But my old flame Erica
Last seen in America
It was a night to be excited

Danny did his tricks
Keeping the crowd transfixed
In the Christopher Creek boozer
He laughed and joked
And some he provoked
All the ladies hoped he'd choose her

That line makes no sense
Our feelings were immense

*As in walked Keith and Rita*
*Danny's lovely Colette*
*Need fear no threat*
*For he's no interest in young senoritas*

*Down Old Christchurch Road*
*The crowd of us strode*
*A long time since we've done that*
*The Chinese was good*
*But in all likelihood*
*It wasn't as good as the chit-chat*

*Hungover next morning*
*Sue woke me with a warning*
*I was supposed to have a coffee with Mark*
*I dragged myself out of bed*
*Sea air cleared my head*
*It was worth getting up with the larks*

*Friday was just a dry run*
*For we'd only begun*
*To enjoy our weekend in Bournemouth*
*Arrangements complete*
*A quick bite to eat*
*Nothing to be unsure about*

*The place was the best*
*And Danny was set*
*Ninety best friends soon arrived*
*The music was flowing*
*Faces were glowing*
*Our friendships were all revived*

*Now you might not believe me*
*And that won't displease me*
*For I know exactly what you're thinking*
*If you haven't kept in touch*

*You can't mean so much*
*And it's only because you're all drinking*

*Well you've got it all wrong*
*Our friendship's still strong*
*For we lived through so much in the past*
*We shared our nightmares*
*And we had our affairs*
*But tonight we were having a blast*

*We were all so excited*
*But some weren't invited*
*They'd never been part of our scene*
*So Dave and I worked the door*
*As we'd discussed before*
*Last night as we ate our chow mein*

*For those who weren't invited*
*You may be feeling slighted*
*But this wasn't for the flotsam and Jetsam*
*Or those turning up in a Stetson*
*It was for special friends reunited*

*So if you weren't part of our crowd*
*In '76 when we were so proud*
*You should be aware*
*That we didn't want you there*
*And through the door you weren't allowed*

*Dave Brotherton and Dave Adams*
*(With his fists like a cannon)*
*Were just about the first to arrive*
*Maria and Lorraine*
*Fab to see again*
*Yet they only looked twenty-five!*

*My old mate Laine*

68

*We've always maintained*
*Our love would last forever*
*She's like a sister to me*
*I'm sure she'd agree*
*We're here for each other whatever*

*At the bar it was my call*
*And Sue was welcomed by all*
*For to wives & husbands we're all friendly*
*Danny played all the sounds*
*Of old Bournemouth Town*
*What an amazingly special assembly*

*Then in walked Roger Ryder*
*Drinking his cider*
*So great to see my old mate*
*And next I saw Kitch*
*Who was born in a ditch*
*This was cause to celebrate.*

*The Hughes Corporation*
*For our generation*
*Who can forget "Do the Hustle'?*
*Or 'Zing Went the Strings …'*
*When we were all kings*
*And we all had much more muscle*

*Erica and Trish*
*Both looking so swish*
*Came and joined us at the bar*
*Then Sandy and Steve*
*I couldn't believe*
*That us rogues had all come so far.*

*We think it's Tourette's*
*That without any regrets*
*Over his head Dave throws his own beer*

His aim's getting better
He soaked his new sweater
But Dave's always full of good cheer

And good to see Mick
Used to his brother's tricks
As is his lovely wife Nicky
The Brothos are a family
With a sense of pageantry
And Maria's passed her looks onto Carley

The lovely Pam, Lynsie and Janice
Could make the blues banish
And don't forget the gorgeous Colette
Or the beautiful Maxine
Looking like a May Queen
And that's not even the whole set

Melanie from The Buccaneer
I thought that she'd disappeared
But old friends kept coming through the door
In walked Brian Omar
Who said he wouldn't roam far
What else did this night have in store?

I'll tell you, Rod Lamont
Fresh in from Vermont
And also Joe Harris
Who'd arrived from Paris
I can't name all ninety
I'd need the Almighty

We bought Danny a watch
'cos he doesn't drink Scotch
And he got ever so slightly emotional
And Maria baked the cake
With a deckchair as a keepsake

*For Danny, it was just as sociable*

*Forty years in the making*
*It was truly breath-taking*
*But what makes this reunion unique*
*Were the times we shared.*
*You can't compare*
*To a school reunion so bleak*

*You see when you were at school*
*Your mates were quite cool*
*But others just empty vessels*
*We're the chosen ones*
*Who despite blows and bums*
*Set out to make our life special*

*A week or two afterwards I went out for a pint and a curry with a couple of pals, and the conversation turned to the party weekend. When I tried to explain how magical it was I could see a little scepticism in their eyes. My mate Pete said, "If I hadn't seen someone for five years, it would be kind of interesting to bump into them again, good to see how they're getting on. If I hadn't seen them for ten years, then I figure we'd probably lost touch for a reason. But if I hadn't seen them for twenty or thirty years then it's unlikely we'll have anything left in common. We may have enjoyed each other's company back in the day, but that was then and this is now, and taking into consideration everything that's gone on in-between, raising families and such like, I honestly don't think I'd want to see those people now."*

*"You've got it all wrong," I replied, "Back in Bournemouth, and travelling abroad together like we did, we shared so much and lived in other's pockets (for want of a better expression) so much that we learned to stick together. We had each other's backs then, and we've got each other's backs right now, 30-40 years later."*

*How amazing is that! How special is that!*

*But allow me to share an understanding of where my friend's coming from, and why this was so different from your average school reunion. You see, when you go to school, you're thrown into a room with thirty other kids. You have very little choice about this. Maybe you know a few from your old school, or from a football team, but chances are you'll make other mates. You like some of those thirty kids, and others you haven't got a lot of time for because you're all so different. You got to kind of kick along with them because, as I said, you had no choice. And for the most part when you leave school you all go your separate ways.*

*And then someone organises a school reunion. Well, you didn't like them back then, and, let's face it, you don't really like them much now, and that's why my mate says that "you probably lost touch for a reason."*

*It's the same with people at work actually. They're not your mates. They're your work-mates, your colleagues, and that's as far as it goes.*

*But with us it's different. When we aimed ourselves towards Bournemouth in the late '70s and early '80s (for me it was '76) we were searching for kindred spirits, fellow adventurers, people who wanted to live off their wits and who wanted to have fun while they did so.*

*You didn't choose who you went to school with, and you don't choose who you work with, but back in '76 we chose each other. And we weathered the storms together. Work mates won't do that for you.*

*"I used to think I was the strangest person in the world, but then I thought, there are so many people in the world, there must be someone just like me who feels bizarre and flawed in the same ways I do. I would imagine her and imagine that she must be out there thinking of me too. Well, I hope that if you are out there you read this and know that yes, it's true I'm here, and I'm just as strange as you." Frida Kahlo*

*And then I went down to Bournemouth and found them. And guess what, they're just as nutty as me, some more so.*

*We're the black sheep, the rejects, the bizarre and outlandish. We're flawed, and we fall down the cracks, but we're never forgotten.*

*What people don't realise, though, is that we have the most beautiful souls.*

# 23.     Further note from Karl - We didn't shake hands

*You see, even though a lot of us have travelled in different directions, and it was important that we did so, and even though we all have other mates, and rightly so, our group are special, because at our reunion on Saturday 25th November 2017, with Danny doing what he does best, the conversation never, ever dried up. We spoke about the fun we had and we spoke about our flaws. We talked about lies we've told, the hells we've seen, our childhood, our adventures, what keeps us up at night, our self-doubts and fears, and how we all admitted to feeling butterflies in our stomach that night. We hugged each other and spoke with intensity, with affection and excitement, and with twisted minds.*

*What we didn't do was shake hands and say, "Alright?"*

*That's for school reunions.*

*We probably held hands a lot, I know I did. I held Laine's hand a lot, and I held Erica's hand a lot, and I hugged a lot of other people. I guess I just wanted to be sure they were actually there after all these years, although I've seen Laine a couple of times in the last year or so.*

*But we didn't shake hands.*

*Why? Because everything was so intense. Everything seemed to take on new and deeper meanings. We do the world no favours by waiting at bus stops (metaphorically speaking), by not rocking the boat and by pretending that what's inside of all of us isn't mind-boggling!*

*This is why I say, nutty philosopher that I am, that our 'tribe' is coming back together again. We've completed two-thirds of our Earthwalk, and at times it's been tough, but we're still standing, aren't we?*

*I can only recall my own memories. Back in '76 I shared a room with Danny in the Palace Chambers. And it was here I met Erica, who stuck with me through thick and thin, including a winter in a tent in the middle of the Forêt de St-Germain, just outside Paris, followed by hitch-hiking through France and Spain to reach Benidorm where, as is the nature of 'seasonal' workers the world over, we found work in night clubs and discos.*

*My first job when we got to California was working on the door at The King's Head, which I did for a few months and then a few of us found work at The Meatless Messhall, a vegetarian restaurant. I was assistant manager, in charge of the chicken and ribs window and the hotdog* truck. I know, I know, it's a vegetarian restaurant, but this was California.

Danny was originally working there but was forced to leave. He'd had a fight with a Chicano. A few members of a gang called the Venice Sho-Line, who the year before had iced ten blacks in ten days, had come into the restaurant late at night. I'm not too sure how it started but Danny had ended up beating the crap out of one of them. It wasn't an easy fight though, and he'd come away quite marked up himself, but he has Gypsy blood in him and a Gypsy's no slouch in a tear-up.

Whatever, it was a bad career move. You know the Chicano type – Latin American descent, slicked-back hair, tiny goatee beards, tattoos of the Madonna or a Crucifix on their chests. They used to always dress in white tank tops. And when it comes to trouble, it's very much a macho thing with them. They will win, whatever. If you were to beat one of them in a fair fight, as Danny had, then he'd come back and knife you. If you took the knife off him then he'd come back and shoot you. They must win. Very scary.

This guy who Danny beat had threatened to come back with a gun and carry him out in a paper bag. It unnerved Danny enough for him to quit the job immediately.

*I lasted three years in California, and then it was back to Bournemouth for a couple more years, mostly working the doors and building sites.*

*After that I was back out to America, although I went on the road, travelling the States for five years altogether, but that's another story. I am, however, so delighted to know that Danny and the others made a success of their lives out there. There's a part of me that wishes I'd stayed. We were poor in pocket but rich in spirit. However, if I had stayed I wouldn't have met my wife Sue, our son Kai wouldn't exist, and we wouldn't have the solid family unit that we now have. And that means more to me than anything. Absolutely anything.*

*Times were often hard, but one thing that never left us was the Heaven-sent ability to laugh at ourselves. Looking back, we had a light-hearted acceptance of our poverty and hard life. Our sense of humour never deserted us.*

*I'm proud of that. And like I said above I'm so proud of the fact that my mates and the others have made a success of their lives out there*

*So what brought our 'tribe' back together after we all truly believed that strong as the memories are our true friends had all wandered away through the mists of time. Danny's birthday? Lorraine's party in Essex earlier in the year? Or cosmic forces beyond  our understanding?*

It was Paulo Coelho, the author who wrote that great book 'The Alchemist,' who said, "Important encounters are planned by the souls long before the bodies see each other."

And I kind of like to believe that, although of course I can't prove it.

Mind you, you can't prove it's not true, so …..

Either way, these are the people who shaped me.

I love chaotic people, People who don't fit in a box or stay between the lines, but whose integrity is greater than any rule book and whose loyalty is stronger than blood.

When I look at the photographs from our reunion party, every last one of us has a spark of mischief in our eyes, and that spark of mischief is what connects us all. Not everybody has this. But we're Carefree Scamps, all of us. And we make people laugh.

There's something about certain people's chosen 'lifestyle' which ages them. I can't explain it any other way. Leaving school, building a career, getting old before their time as they take on more stress lacks that one essential element that Danny and all of our 'Tribe' had oodles of as youngsters, and that's fun. We had lively, buoyant and animated fun. We were carefree at an age when you're supposed to be carefree. We were breezy, jaunty and happy-go-lucky.

The flip side of this is that at times it may make some of us feel as if we're outsiders. People occasionally talk about us in hushed tones, whispering that we're a bit of a lone wolf, or at times a loose cannon. They don't want to say it to our faces because every now and again we can be a little bit unpredictable. But they look at us with a strange curiosity, because in comparison – although they're often very successful at 'fitting in' – these people lead lives that are drab, dreary and monotonous. They're not unruly like us. We have a divine spark of unruliness within us. And it's that unruliness which has kept us young.

To misquote environmentalist, David W. Orr, "the earth does not need more prosperous, wealthy and fortunate people. The earth desperately needs more philosophers and Shamans, more sweethearts, more artists and DJs, more Gypsies and more tattooed storytellers."

What the world is absolutely crazed for right now is people like Danny, existing in the most genuine and exquisitely candid and honourable version of himself.

This is why we're here. All of us. To make the world smile.

The three-day reunion and combination birthday celebration is all the evidence Danny needs of just how many hearts he has touched in his 60 years.

*And he does this simply by being Danny. He is, it has to be said, an old soul*

*The earth is full of fake people, but Danny has the inspiration of a jester, the heart and soul of a warrior and the loyalty of a puppy, and he draws people to him through his love and honesty. With all the savagery and broken dreams, this is still a wonderful world*

# 24. Arribada by Karl Wiggins

*Our son, Kai, backpacked around Central America for 8 months, working in bars in Guatemala and Mexico, spending a whole month in El Salvador and picking up his scuba diving tickets (Open Water and Advanced) in Honduras. In Costa Rica there is just one beach that year after year sea turtles return to in order to lay their eggs. There's about 10,000 miles of coastline, yet the turtles find the very same beach year after year. This is called the arribada and is apparently one of the world's most spectacular displays as hundreds of thousands of turtle's eggs are laid under the new moon.*

*To put this into perspective, males never leave the ocean, and females only come ashore to lay their eggs on sandy beaches during the nesting season, and that's not until the sea turtle has reached adulthood (3-5 years). In the meantime, they spend most of their time floating on seaweed mats, in which they find shelter and food. Sea turtles migrate thousands of miles in their lifetime through ocean basins and high seas. They often undergo long migrations, some as far as 12,000 miles, between their feeding grounds and the beaches where they nest. One female leatherback was tracked travelling more than 14,000 miles roundtrip across the Pacific*

*Ocean, from Papua in Indonesia to the northwest coast of the United States.*

*And yet when it's time to lay their eggs, the females come back to the very same beach they first hatched at, on a coastline 10,000 miles long.*

*They can only be using some kind of magnetic field imprinted in their brains as they leave the nest.*

*A bit like our tribe, if you like, returning to Bournemouth*

*AS I SAID ABOVE, YOU'RE PROBABLY WONDERING WHAT THIS HAS TO DO WITH ANXIETY AND DEPRESSION?*

*AND I ASKED YOU TO STAY WITH ME, BECAUSE I'VE BEEN GOING SOMEWHERE WITH ALL THIS*

*YOU SEE, LESS THAN A YEAR AFTER OUR BOURNEMOUTH REUNION, ONE OF US WAS SAVAGELY MURDERED IN THE MOST BRUTAL FASHION IN AN UNPROVOKED AND GROUNDLESS ATTACK*

*IT HIT ALL OF US HARD, BUT WAS THE START OF DANNY'S DEPRESSION ….. TO ADD TO HIS ANXIETY*

*SO AS WELL AS EXPERIENCING SUDDEN JITTERS, DANNY ALSO STARTED TO GENERATE*

*EMOTIONS SUCH AS HELPLESSNESS AND OUTRAGE*

*ANXIETY AND DEPRESSION; THE FRATERNAL TWINS OF MOOD DISORDERS AND CHAOS*


*ALMOST A YEAR TO THE DAY WE ALL MET AGAIN, BUT THIS TIME FOR A MUCH SADDER REASON; CHALKIE'S FUNERAL*

# PART TWO

## Murder

# 25.    Murder

My world fell apart in one phone call, and it was then announced by Dave the Boxer on our group chat page; "This is probably one of the hardest, saddest things that I have ever been asked to do. Yesterday at approximately 2 p.m. a knife-wielding maniac took the life of my best mate and broke my heart. He was simply going about his job and someone decided to end his life prematurely for absolutely no reason. We are devastated"

# 26.    Grief

I'm fully aware of real friends and acquaintances but having said that it's great to talk to people when grief knocks on your door. I grew up like Peter Pan and laughed my way through life. Life was brilliant! Young, free and, of course, making friends. But I was like a butterfly and flew from flower to flower and never thought that there were certain flowers that were sweeter and more beautiful, warm and colourful, and whose petals reached out and held me. They made life wonderful and were always there for me. Even rain could not stop this flower from embracing me through 42 years.

Then one day my flower died. Cut down. And I have never felt so much sadness. I have to talk about my flower.

I'm talking, of course, about my best friend, Chalkie, who was killed. He was a plumber, and he just went out to do a job in London and ended up killed by a madman.

When the news came in it hit me so hard that my life had no meaning. All friends in the UK were in disbelief, and his wife, as you can imagine, was inconsolable. We were all in total shock, including Dave the Boxer and Lorraine, and Paul, Lorraine's brother. Dave has known Chalkie since they were kids, they were like brothers, both sharpening their skills together in boxing gyms and getting up to all sorts of mischief. The love between them was as if they really were brothers.

I have a chance here in this book to say thank you to all who contacted me and helped me get through a really bad time. I dreaded the flight home to bury my best friend and what awaited us all when we said goodbye. It was only a few months previously that we were dancing at the Bournemouth reunion party. For those who never got to meet him, he was a man's man, a gentleman. He reminded me of my cousin, Paul, who also left us way too soon. Gentle, kind and you just fell in love with him once you met him.

I'm not asking for pity when I write this. God, that's such a weak emotion. No, I'm writing this as a recognition and tribute to my best friend. It helps me to talk about him and those who knew him know exactly what I'm saying. The church was packed and the heartbreak is still felt coast to coast. He meant so much to so many people. He was a film director, writer, even a poet. He was very quiet with a heart of gold. Everyone shares my pain, I know, but as Karl says, "Now, even more than ever, we must all stick together. We shared so much and lived in other's pockets so much that we learned to stick together. We lived together, worked together, socialised together and loved together. We had each other's backs then, and we've got each other's backs right now, 30-40 years later."

How special is that! We'll help each other to carry on. I still have a garden of wonderful flowers and cherish every one of them even more. Once I get my butterfly wings back I will fly again to each of my flowers and take time to kiss each one them

Thank you all for my garden

Never take someone for granted. Hold all your true friends close to your heart because you might wake up one day and realise you've lost a diamond when you were too busy collecting pebbles.

Never in my life have I ever felt such grief, sadness, anguish, despondency, rage, wretchedness and heartbreak all rolled into one. And the same question keeps popping up. Why? Why why why why why? As his wife says, "The nutcase that did this to him would have loved him in different circumstances." Such a sad, senseless waste of a beautiful man taken too soon.

# 27.    A note from Karl

*It may seem impersonal not to mention our friend's name, but at time of writing the trial for his killer is on the horizon, and the jury will be expected to decide based purely on the evidence they hear in court, as well as the arguments from the prosecution, defence and directions from the judge. If the jury reads something anywhere which hasn't been presented in court, the defendant has no opportunity to present a defence, which could adversely impact the verdict of the case*

*In 2015, two teenage girls (aged 13 and 14) were accused of murdering a vulnerable alcoholic woman from Hartlepool. Before the second day of the trial was out, there were more than 500 comments on Facebook. Some threatened the accused, others scoffed at their pleas of innocence and others attacked the court process itself. The judge concluded that the jurors would not be able to deliver a verdict solely based on the evidence presented in court and SCRAPPED THE TRIAL.*

*A second trial was set and at a later date the girls received life sentences with a minimum of 15 years each.*

So in our friend's killer's trial, what we don't want is for the defendant's lawyer to discover comments in books or on social media about the situation, resulting in this trial being scrapped as well. In fact, the Contempt of Court Act 1981 makes it an offence to publish anything which could prejudice a trial.

Not only are printed comments likely to prejudice the trial, but as members of the general public we're less likely to be aware of the law and risks of prejudicing a trial, meaning we're more likely to end up in contempt of court. In 2011 a woman juror, Joanne Frail, was jailed for 8 months for contacting a defendant by Facebook. Unbelievably stupid I know, but there you have it.

I spoke to Danny and Dave the Boxer and, for these reasons, we all feel it's extremely important that our friend's name is kept out of all published material (books or social media) until after the trial. And for quite a while afterwards

All of us believe that if there is even the remotest of chance that anything could jeopardise this trial, and the conviction of this man, then all precautions should be taken.

## 28.    Dental Costs

I was dealing with personal sadness at home in the UK and trying to keep going and stay positive. And as my dad used to say, as one door closes, another door opens. Our thoughts are now with our lovely Brenda's family. We all prayed for her recovery, but she too walked the stairway to heaven

I always thought life was a piece of cake!

It's really not, is it? It's a journey that has so many twists and turns and heartbreak and sadness, but we all keep going and the world turns, and we thank God we're healthy.

As most of us struggle with bloody bills and worries, the cost of living here in California is getting worse week by week. So fast forward ...... dental work is so expensive here. Robbing bastards. I went to my local dentist here and they wanted $16,000 – yes, you read it right $16,000 (£12,675) - to do root canals, bridges, caps, crowns etc

I would have to sleep with my head in a safe

So, thank goodness my good friend, Bolton Steve, took me to Mexico for the day. OMG, I had four major fillings, one crown and a cleaning. All that for $400. That's right, $400. You leave

Santa Monica at 5am, you're in the chair in Mexico by 8am, they drill for the crown and take impressions and you then go shopping or have a few drinks. Then three hours later you come back, get fitted with a new porcelain crown. That costs $150. The fillings cost $50 each, so if you want info on the greatest dentist, just contact me and I'll pass on the information. Make a day of it. You can even take the train.

Big hug and thanks to Bolton Steve, heart of a lion, thank you so much. Here a crown alone costs ten times that amount. You do the maths

Love ya

# 29. I Turned into a Lunatic

I don't know what happened. And I don't know why it happened. Well, I obviously do, but I didn't know you could turn into a lunatic just like that. I took off all my clothes, just had my boxers on and walked all the way down to the Meatless Messhall on Venice Beach, where I used to work with Karl a lifetime ago.

I had no money, no phone and bare feet. I was totally lost

I feel a lot better now, but it was very, very scary. Can you lose your mind just like that?

# 30.  Can you Really Lose Your Mind? (by Karl)

*If you know Danny, or if you've known him, you'd never believe it but he's starting to suffer social anxiety. If he has to go to an event he finds so many excuses not to go.*

*I know someone who suffers from S.A.D., which I always thought was bollocks because in the UK we live in rainy country. We're used to it. But she was in tears explaining it to me. And she explained about how it's all about loss; loss of the summer, loss of the daylight hours, loss of the leaves as they fall. While most of us enjoy the autumnal colours as the leaves fall, for her it involves debilitating feelings of loss.*

*I think the challenges Danny's facing now, as I said in my forward, are also to do with loss. Loss of his parents. Loss of youth. Loss of youthful good looks. Loss of his friend through a savage murder. Loss of his hair even. Perhaps even 'fear' of loss of income for any of a dozen reasons, but certainly loss, as his children move away and get on with their lives. Yet Danny and his beautiful wife, Colette, are obviously terrific parents because they've given their kids both roots and wings.*

In that case, the only antidote would be some kind of gain or acquisition. That might be a boost.

Easy to say, though, isn't it?

When he's behind the DJ stand, that's his comfort blanket. Playing to the crowd. Danny is a phenomenal DJ. He's THE English DJ in Los Angeles. Back when we were teenagers with the world at our feet Danny was the one who made everyone laugh …. But I was the one who made him laugh. Someone has to make the comedian laugh, right? And I'm proud to call him brother.

But now we're in our 60's and neither of us, or any of our friends, know how that happened. How did we go from being teenagers to being 60?

I don't know.

The problem with being the class clown is not that everybody expects it from you all the time, because they don't, the problem is that the class clown 'thinks' everyone else expects it from them all the time.

So while the DJ stand is Danny's comfort blanket – he loves doing magic tricks etc. – it's his mask. When Danny's DJing a party he's hiding behind that mask, and no one senses his agony.

*Walking into a social event can't be easy when you just want to be you, but you've worn that mask for so long that it's become almost like a knight's shiny armour that has rusted in place and can't be removed. Our Earthwalk is naturally filled with hope and despair, belief and disillusionment, laughter and tears – all of us – and while Danny has spent his life slaying dragons and rescuing damsels in distress (metaphorically), he's become famous for his armour, which has always been so shiny. But he's now worn his armour so long that he fears his friends have forgotten how he looks without it.*

*But we haven't.*

*You see, Danny's REAL friends understand that Generalised Anxiety Disorder, which is the flash new term for it, is not just "being a bit anxious." You can't just "chill out a bit" or "get over it". It eats into your comfort and contentment and your total belief in yourself.*

*When someone suffering from anxiety issues calls off, or ducks out, or makes what you might think is a feeble excuse, please try and appreciate that it isn't personal, it isn't apathy or unwillingness to be part of what's going on. That person is not being disrespectful. It's because they can't physically do it.*

*When someone needs encouragement, or a bit of hand-holding, they're not being feeble or immature, and they're certainly not trying to elicit attention. It's because they are frantic to beat it, but they can't do it on their own.*

*You see, Danny's not troubled by genuine difficulties or dilemmas, although you might think he is. No, Danny's more troubled by his imagined anxieties about genuine difficulties or dilemmas. Does that make sense?*

*They give him the jitters.*

*Have you ever arranged a coffee or a glass of Prosecco with friends, or planned to go to football with boys, and all of a sudden the four walls you occupy seems to be your only sanctuary, because it's the only place you feel safe, the only place you don't have to fake being okay, so you cancel?*

*You feel like you're going back on your word, but that's all you can do.*

*Or how about when you're invited to do something socially, and you're all full of remorse and apologetic and contrite because you have to explain that you've already booked up that weekend, when in reality you're standing on an island and burning all your bridges?*

*So what happens next? I'll tell you. People stop asking you and the isolation that at first wasn't valid becomes your only reality.*

*Don't be afraid to leave the castle. You're wanted. You're the only you there is. It's a great big world out there. Enjoy it!*

*And for those readers fortunate enough not to suffer this mental illness, please don't give up on your friends. We're all weird and damaged in our own way. But friends suffering from anxiety or depression aren't freaks. Ring them, go around, even when they don't want you to. Because they really do want you to, they just don't know how to say it.*

*Danny's poetry is sometimes very, very good - exceptionally so in fact - but sometimes it's shit. And that's okay. A lot of my writing is shit too. But all the false adulation he gets for it, all those people who blow smoke up his arse saying, "Oh Danny Danny Danny, that's wonderful, why don't you publish a book?" when in reality it's a bit depressing, aren't helping.*

*And when he did publish a book – or rather when I published it with his name on the cover (it's called 'Bournemouth Boys and Boscombe Girls' by the way and is brilliant!) – none of them bought it. Why? Because despite all this "Oh Danny Danny Danny" bullshit none of them really mean it.*

*They're all full of shit!*

*WE mean it, his REAL friends, and that includes everyone who was at our friend's funeral; Dave Adams, Lorraine, Dave Brotherton, Maria Brotherton, Roger, Colette, Cherry, Steve Wheelband, Tony Caves, Giggy, Laine, all the people who've shared a lifetime with Danny and know the stories that certainly can't be printed. But not those pricks on Facebook who pretend to love him when they don't even know him. They don't mean it. They're full of shit.*

*And why do I understand all that? Because I'm a bit like Danny. With certain friends I have to be the class clown because it's expected of me ……..* "What can I say to be funny?"

*It's not easy, and everyone's entitled to a meltdown every now and again. But the important thing is not to unpack your bags and live there.*

*Both Danny and Colette have my empathy, my support and my love. If you ever feel like you're losing everything, remember that trees lose their leaves every year and yet they still stand tall waiting for better things to come.*

*Danny's fortunate, of course, in that he has the love and support of his beautiful wife, Colette*

# 31.　　In Fact, I'm not Finished Yet (by Karl)

*I just wish more people would appreciate it. What Danny has is not heartburn or indigestion. And he won't get better immediately. A nap's not going to help. He is not lazy or indifferent, but he is exhausted and weary to the point where he may appear too laid back. He's on the sweets already, on some kind of anti-anxiety tablets. I don't know what they are. Some American thing, I suppose. Medication to make it easier for him to thrive and not merely endure. If you didn't know him, you'd think he's faking it or that whatever it is he'll just have to deal with it. That's like telling a deaf person to listen harder. You see, sometimes Danny's able to push through the pain, but there are days when his head's spinning so fast that he can't even walk. His whole torso is physically and mentally injured. His state of mind fluctuates and he's unhappy a lot. Sick at heart. He tries to control these breakneck changes in mood. However, when mood swings are so powerful that they cause confusion, he starts to suffer from depression and even some kind of bipolar disorder. During manic periods, he may become reckless and volatile, such as taking off all his clothes and walking to Venice Beach barefoot. He takes his medication and many vitamins every day, plus he does his yoga, and for the most part that keeps him 'up' but some days nothing works.*

*It's all just emptiness.*

## 32.   Harpie

*I'm still not finished (Karl).*

*With her full permission, I'm going to share some excerpts from the diary of a close friend of mine, Harpie, just to demonstrate what can really go wrong when people start to feel depressed. Harpie used to cut herself, you see. And not like those 'silly little Emo children, making pathetic little cat scratches on their arms, flaunting what they're doing to the rest of the world' either. No, Harpie cut deep.*

*As far as I know, no one (except for Harpie) has ever discussed the deep shame, the reasons behind self-mutilation and how this extremely unsound way of confronting emotional pain, acute anger or resentment is far from a joke.*

## 33.     23rd January 2005 by Harpie;

I met John, man number three, last Saturday. Oh boy, what a charmer he was. This one had no qualms about my getting there under my own steam; neither did he offer to pick me up, just the reverse. He expected me to pick him up from The Island - which is miles away. His house was amazing, he had a gold Jaguar parked in the drive next to the speed boat. Before he even answered the door, I knew that we weren't going to get on. I don't do flash and pretentious. John's business was in car dealership and he wasn't doing badly.

I knocked at the door. Instead of answering it he appeared from around the back and told me to follow him. He led me to the back door along a muddy path. I had to bend down and rescue my satin stiletto heel from a quagmire of mud. It was pitch black and I couldn't see where I was going. It was raining hard. I was surprised when he told me that he wasn't ready and would be a couple of minutes. He shut the back door in my face and left me standing out in the rain. I couldn't believe how rude he was and contemplated getting back in my car and driving away - but at least one of us has manners.

True to his word he wasn't long, and we set off.

Far from being a snob he was just the opposite. Twat was among his favourite words, he had several others in his repertoire all with the suffix of fucking. I can't stand foul-mouthed people who swear in every sentence through sheer habit. Swearing doesn't bother me but when people use them in every sentence, they're making up for something. Being thick, I suppose. And they're trying to show off, 'Look at me, I use swear words. I'm hard and I'm a Jack the lad. See how comfortable I am using 'shit' and 'fuck' and 'bollocks' I'm Jack. Aren't you impressed?'

Not really.

When we got to the pub he called me a tight bastard because I told him that I object to paying for the expensive vodka and normally get the house double if I haven't brought my own bottle out. I object to being called a bastard. I told him that we don't all own gold Jaguars and speed boats. Throughout the course of the evening he brought the subject around to my 'tits' several times. He had an ingenious knack of turning almost any conversation around to the subject of tits. It was a party piece. He told me out of the blue that he has a large penis; I assume that is in compensation for his lack of social skills.

Looks-wise he was shorter than me and said that tall women are a huge turn on. He was bald, bespectacled and had a face that only a mother could love, but he wasn't all bad. He did have some charm. I don't suppose he could have attained his financial status if he didn't have some people skills. He drank heavily all night and got louder with every drink until I was cringing. I can mix in any circles. We weren't anywhere classy or posh, just in my local so he didn't embarrass me, I just couldn't stand his lack of manners. I made the best of a poor situation and didn't have too bad a night. He was impressed when Kenny's Trollop, Venereal Val, as I call her, came up and tried to warn me off Kenny. He said afterwards that he thought there was going to be a cat fight between us. He was disappointed that I walked away from her.

At the end of the night I had to laugh. He told me that he could get a drink in any pub after last orders, 'You just have to know how to talk to the bar tottie, don't you?' He did the poorest imitation of a John Travolta swagger that I've ever seen. 'So, darling` am I alright for a drink, or what?'

'No.'

'Oh.'

Without another word, he walked meekly back to his seat forgetting all about his swagger. The funniest thing was that the pub will have carried on serving until the early hours and he is the only person I've ever known to be refused. It amused the hell out of me.

'So, what are we going to do now, then?' he asked, suggestively, he was dripping sleaze and even if I was into casual sex, I'd rather have cut my arm off than shag him.

'Well I could invite you back to mine for a coffee.'

His eyes lit up.

'But I'm not going to because I don't think you'd understand the concept of coffee without a leg over on the side, so I'm going to thank you for the night out and say Goodnight.'

We were standing outside on the square. He looked horrified that he'd put in the groundwork all night and was getting the brush off.

'Right then,' he said, 'I'm off to Barran to try my luck there.' They were his exact words and his tone was nasty.

Gail, a barmaid I know, was climbing into her taxi home, and he yelled out to her, 'Hey lass, are you going to Barran? Can I share your taxi? I'm off down Gaza Street to pull.'

He jumped in her taxi and off they went. He left me standing on the square without so much as a thank you, a goodbye, a kiss-my-arse or a single wasted word. Obviously, the man was a cretin and I didn't give a shit about him, but it did have an effect on me.

I felt worthless again. I felt small and used and dirty. How could somebody have such a low opinion of me that they could treat me with such disrespect? I felt like going home and cutting myself - I've done that before, and it's never pretty - so I did the sensible thing and called at Megan's so she could talk me down. She was asleep. I had no choice but to go home. The house was cold and empty, I felt alone and lonely, but I resisted the scissors.

# 34.    5th July 2005 by Harpie:

It's two o'clock in the morning and I can't sleep so I've come to write instead. It's more than that, I need to write. If I don't, I'm going to take a pair of scissors and cut myself. During difficult feelings and overwhelming situations, I cut myself. I feel better, and I can cope for a while. I'm ashamed of it. But getting the tainted blood out is often the only way I can deal with emotional pain. I don't slice myself for attention, I work hard to hide it. It's abhorrent and everything about the outside me is concerned with showing the world how normal and stable I am. Ninety nine percent of the time I succeed too.

I'm weak. But I feel as though my blood's screaming as it moves around my body and the only way to release the scream is to release the blood. I see it as black and dirty and when these feelings come on me, it only gets blacker and dirtier. It makes me feel sick having the diseased blood inside me. It doesn't stop. It's been building up for days, and tonight I want to cut myself.  This is my way of dealing with the screaming blood. But I learned a couple of years ago that writing to my diary can curb the urge until it passes. It's a new way to channel the black stuff.

As a child, whenever I felt worthless, or dirty, or useless I'd punish myself with a pair of scissors. It became an addiction and although I've only cut myself once in the last fifteen years - about four years ago - sometimes the urge is so fucking strong. It's got nothing to do with the cutting or hurting myself. It's a screwed up, fucked up need to get rid of my dirty blood so that it can regenerate with new, clean blood. When I'm down and feeling like a worthless piece of shit, I get it into my head that my blood is dirty. It's a visualisation. I can see it in my mind's eye as something black and coiled, spiralling through my body and poisoning me. I'm a rational, sensible woman, I know that it's stupid and something that is purely of my own pathetic imagination. But I can't get rid of those feelings. It's as strong as any addiction. And apart from that one blip a few years back, I'm proud of myself that it's something I've overcome and got the better of. Writing has helped me and given me something else to channel the bad feelings into. It doesn't stop the visualisation, but it enables me to not act on the compulsion.

These silly little Emo children annoy me. They make their pathetic little cat scratches on their arms and then parade around, showing them to the world. 'Look at me, Look at me, see my pain.' They scratch words like 'Hurting' into their skin, no deeper than a kitten could inflict and flaunt what they're doing to the world. Half of them have no pain to flaunt, so they invent it because they're part of this weak-arsed culture group where they're all supposed to be EMOtionally unstable. To prove it, they scratch their arms.

They are emotionally flaccid.

I have never felt more shame than after I've cut. Nobody except my niece knows. I wore long sleeves and bandaged tightly to hide what I'd done. It wasn't for attention it was to get rid of the dirty blood. I used to cut deep into the veins in my arms, it was a ritual. I had a special pair of scissors that I'd sharpen for an hour beforehand in the hope that the compulsion would subside but sharpening only heightened it. I never used anything else. I had a white enamelled bowl and I'd hold my arms high and let the filthy blood pour down to my elbows and drain into the basin until I was close to unconsciousness and I had to tourniquet my arms before I passed out. I'd often have to stitch the wounds myself. I was too ashamed to go to hospital. Sometimes that wasn't enough, and I'd lie in an empty bath and open my femoral artery. It got to this stage when I was training to be a nurse. I brought suturing kits home, I didn't steal them, I just brought them home for personal use. I saved the tax payer hundreds of pounds by self-suturing. I'd open the same wound every time, three stitches long, the artery is permanently damaged, and I have a hole in the muscle that I can fit the end of my finger into.

As well as opening veins in my arms and legs, I used to hack at my boobs. I'm heavy-breasted and hate them. It was dangerous because my compulsion would go out of control. I used to fantasise about pulling out my nipples and cutting them off with the scissors. I made deals with myself, 'Okay you can do your arms and leg and boobs but leave the nipples alone, right?' It wasn't cowardice that stopped me from doing it. I have a high tolerance to pain and was filled with self-loathing. Not doing it was almost impossible, but something in me knew that it was a line I couldn't cross. I might not have succeeded in doing both, but what would be next, cutting off my ears, my fingers, gouging my eyes out? I'd have been locked up.

People have asked me if I've ever suffered from mental illness. I answer no. In my mind it's a truthful answer. I was misdiagnosed as mentally handicapped – as it was called then - when I was a child. Nowadays it's known as emotional collapse, neurasthenia, clinical depression, melancholia, major affective disorder, manic-depressive psychosis, bipolar or just a simple basket case. Everybody dances around the euphemisms, and I can tell you I've got a psychiatric rap-sheet that any decent nutcase would be proud of. But I don't consider myself as ever having a mental illness. It's just that I sometimes feel like I'm a ghost. Not part of the real world at all and as if my mind's been replaced by another type of voice that's stolen all my confidence and told me I'm unworthy of love. Which is probably why my mother was murdered.

It's not the 'blues.' That's when you've just found out your car needs a three-hundred-pound repair job, or you've lost all the contacts from your phone. The difference between people who have the blues and me is that I have compulsions, that's all. I was anorexic for ten years. I cut myself for fifteen. I've spent my whole life fighting for a normal existence, just like everybody else has, but I've never been mentally ill.

Who the fuck am I trying to kid?

I'm talking about mental illness in general. Not about me, I'm fine. In fact, if you didn't know the odd things about me, I'm as sane as the next person in the checkout queue. Other people suffer from it, because it's a culture that's not open to discussion. But I can discuss it, because it's my fucking diary and I can talk about anything I fuckingwellplease. Depression, psychic tension, extreme sadness, despair, inadequacy, they're all illnesses, and mental illness is the only disease that can make you deny its actual existence. Isn't that a frightening thought, that the brain has so much power that it can deny its own illness?

Let's sweep it under the carpet, this mental illness? We'll push it under the radar. 'Get over it, snap yourself out of it,' that's what people say.

Sadness hurts. I have the scars to prove it.

I've been clinically depressed since I was five years old, but I won't admit it. I've never taken anti-depressants in my life. I've never been to a doctor about it. I flatly refuse, that would make me labelled and make me ill. I'm not. I know lots of people on anti-depressants and I think what the fuck have you got to be depressed about with your perfect families and your homes and your jobs?

I know a woman, she's got six perfect children, and they have four perfect grandparents and have stupid names like Lawrence and Sebastian. The girls go to ballet and the boys to karate. The woman is married to the perfect man. They are both professional singers and good enough to afford a six-bedroomed mansion. They drive sports cars. She's stunning with the voice of a professional and has never known a day's financial hardship in her life. Her husband posts pathetic messages on Facebook for her. Baby, you're my world, don't ever leave me because I couldn't live without you. I love you so much. Fuck off. If she had the guts she could do the world a favour and kill herself. Take a look at what you've got and give thanks you selfish, ungrateful, pampered    little fucking princess.

She's my friend, but I suppose after that little rant I despise her. You see, rich people can have nervous breakdowns. They can afford it. But poor people like me can't. I can't have a nervous breakdown, can I? So I used to cut myself, sew myself up and then crawl out of bed the next morning and go to work. That's it.

Each cut is a battle with myself that I've lost, but I don't want to be me anymore

I'm crying as I write this and I'm hurting. Maybe I could cut myself tonight. It'd feel better. It's my fix. I know that this is about me, me, me, but I can only whinge like this to my diary. To everybody else I have to keep my feelings locked away and keep smiling. I pretend to be happy.

I said that writing can curb the urge for a while until I can deal with it.

It didn't.

I'm going to cut myself.

I feel better already.

La la lalalalala la la this isn't mental illness. I'm fine.

And so, so ashamed.

## 35.    Later on, same night, same morning;

My scars are my identity.

I cut myself

For the first time in four years I cut myself, and I hated myself as I did it. All I could think was, I recognise this, I know this, this is familiar.

It's a very matter-of-fact way of hating myself. It's my clemency.

I stood in the bath because I didn't know how deep I was going to cut, or if I'd choose to hack away at my boobs. I stood naked, raised my arms, which lifted my boobs up and I thought about chopping them off with an axe. I attacked the underside of my arm …. Deep, and I hated myself and thought, 'There we go, I'm not a nutcase at all, I'm familiar with this. I'm back in control.'

And the blood spurted with each beat of my heart and poured down my arm and my side and my left tit, and I knew I was in trouble.

The spurting's not good. I cut an artery. I could see yellow-tan lumpy tissue inside my cut and deep red stringy muscle.

I reduced the flow by keeping my arm raised above the level of my heart. I felt weak and cold and knew I had to stitch. I hate myself. I hate myself. I hate myself. I hate myself — I'm fine.

I'm fine

I'm not mad at all. I'm normal. I'm just a little bit further up the road than most people.

I need to keep writing. I'm cleaned and sutured and dressed and everything's wretched in my pathetic, tragic world in which I despise myself, so I need to write.

I should have 'snapped myself out of it' Easy peasy. Why didn't I think of that?

Oh I know, because I'm a weak piece of shit.

Do I need professional help? I don't think I do because I deal with my demons and get on with my life after a wobble. Thank God they are few and far between. Sometimes I just really need a hug. But there's nobody there for me. So tonight, I hugged myself the best way I know how.

I really, really need a hug.

# 36.     29<sup>th</sup> September 2005 by Harpie;

I almost cut myself yesterday after he told me that it was over, and I'd drawn the conclusion that he'd never really cared about me in the first place and that the relationship was just another round of bullshit. The only thing that stopped me is that my son has had my special scissors, the ones I keep for the job and they're as blunt as hell. I was going to do it last night - twice in one year, I haven't done that in a long time - but when I saw the state of them I flung them against the wall before I could do myself any harm. You've no idea what a mess it would make slicing into myself with blunt scissors, and these buggers are blunt as arseholes.

They are still sharp enough to put a hole in the fucking wall though.

And then I got really crazy! I went upstairs to get the set of super sharp chef's knives, but fate intervened again. Thank God fate intervened. I flung open the wardrobe door and remembered that I've already given them away. If those knives had been there I might have done myself some serious permanent damage. That's never been what it's all about. It's not about how much damage I can do, it's not about, 'I'll show them.'

And it's not some warped, attention seeking, emotional blackmail.

It's the opposite, it's furtive and secret and deeply shameful because that's not the person I want the world to see. It's all about the bleeding. In my calm, lucid moments I don't even know what it's all about myself. When I'm in a self-destructive rage, the only person I want to hurt is myself. It's to do with getting the bad blood out, and it's about pain. The sting is acute and when you're hurting physically, it takes your mind off the emotional hurt. I cut myself and let the bad, black, blood flow and with it goes all the pain on the inside.

Isn't that a mature way of dealing with emotional pain, anger and frustration? I'm a fucking whack-job.

It's like all the fucking circuits are fucked up in my fucking brain and all this faulty wiring pushes old scary memories from my subconscious up into my conscious mind. Not the memories themselves, they're always there, poking at me and laughing at me and nudging me, but the anger and sorrow and rage and grief and all those fucked up perceptions and the blood just screams and screams and screeches around my body and …. I just know that if I can hurt myself physically it'll stop.

That's what happens when you have non-consensual sexual incidents with three different men before you're nine years old.

The irony isn't lost on me that even though I've been diagnosed as mentally handicapped myself, I've ended up looking after people with major affective disorders; clinical depressives, and various psychotic maniacs and the like. Somehow, I slipped below the radar. Yet I ask you, who better? Who would understand the issues faced by a bipolar client better than me?

It's like those patronising little shits who spend a couple of hours a week talking down to junkies and alkies, just so they can feel better about themselves and so they can tell everybody what good they're doing, and people can think 'Jolly rah-rah, you're such a special person,' when all they do is interfere for a couple of hours a week instead of allowing people who've been there themselves to do some good. Pious little shits with their grandiose notions of their oh-so-perfect distorted egos.

So who better than an ex-junkie to assist people in going through cold turkey, and who better than me to work with the mentally ill? I'm not and never have been mentally defective. I'm too strong for that, but by God I've teetered on that edge more often than I can count.

People meet me, and they have no idea. I manage my life, my career, my home and my children. I speak eloquently and use proper English. I have intelligence and have used it to spend my entire life hiding who I am and what my father made me.

I thought about hacking at myself with my razor, but it's one of those daft intuition things and there's no denying that when I'm getting ready to go out on a Friday night I can easily make chopped liver out of myself with it. "Intuition: the super lady razor that doesn't cut." Like hell it doesn't. But that wouldn't have been satisfying enough for what I wanted to do to myself.

So I sat on the bed and laughed. Hell, I couldn't even find anything suitable to mutilate myself with. If I had a gun and tried to shoot myself, I'd probably miss my fat arse.

And then the urge was gone, and the shame and loathing slipped in as it always does. And I wished that I'd got one of the super sharp chef's knives to test myself because I know that I wouldn't have done anything with it. It was all just rage and noise and bluster and, two minutes after the storm, I was calm and rational.

I'm not ashamed of self-mutilating; I'm only ashamed of people knowing that I've done it. I didn't know that before now.

This diary is real, this is my life, just as it happens and whatever is lacking in my mental makeup is always going to be lacking, so I'm going to continue meeting men, failing with them and starting out anew.

See, I used to be obese and repulsive. Strangely I never had any trouble finding myself a man, but then the men who I ended up with were real literary characters, arseholes, every last one of them but at least kind of interesting. My life was a shamble, but it made a decent story. Now I've lost most of the excess weight, except for my boobs, and they're huge, and find that Joe Average is coming to my call and so the story just turns in endless circles.

I could save myself some time and write the next twenty romances now. Pick a name, any name, any occupation and body type. I could have sex with every third – no fifth one - the eighth could be a married man, the fourteenth dies in a horrific accident; we haven't had a woman beater for a while, so we'll chuck at least one of those into the equation. The man with three testicles will run off and leave me to bring up his seven kids and the last one will marry me - the last man, that is, not the last kid, or maybe the last kid, if he's old enough - only for me to find out later that he has four other brides lined up that week.  I'll give the book a new name; 'Secrets of a Serial Slut' has a nice ring to it, or 'The Wanton

Whore'. It seems that I'm destined not to find somebody to love.

I really, really need a hug.

## 37.     The First Cut is the Deepest by Danny

Harpie sat beside her mother
And watched her die
The pain that Harpie felt
On that winter's day
Stayed with her throughout her life
And never went away

Her lonely nights of depression
A shadow with many tears
She needed to find some answers
And cure her lonely fears

She looked into her mirror
A reflection of her soul
A pair of scissors in her hand
She suddenly lost control

A bosom of a woman
And looks to quail a tongue
And age was kind to Harpie
A woman to look so young

She closed her eyes with pleasure
A moment of intense pain
And cut her arm with madness
She had only herself to blame

No one saw her illness
She covered her arm and heart
Late at night when demons came
She let the cutting start

One cut deep to the bone

She stitched it with needle and thread
Her demons danced with pleasure
Then whispered in her head

Solitude of a broken mind
The twisted weave she sowed
Her pain she held deep inside
Her mind that lost control

Snow fell on a winter's day
Harpie was all alone
Reflection from her TV screen
Harpie was finally home

A picture hung from a papered wall
A mother and her child
So sad for a little girl
That it was pain that made her smile

Harpie's heart is filled with love
A child that lost her mind
The black screaming blood that tipped the scales
And her scars were left behind

Harpie hasn't cut for many years
In life there are no ifs and buts
Take life one day at a time
For Harpie there were no short Cuts

# 38.    DJ Danny

What happened to the music?
So very long ago
When it had a message
Especially played real slow

Now it's bangs and whistles
Just a constant beat
I do partly agree
That it keeps people on their feet

Drugs played a big part
Like bread and butter
Spreading drugs all night long
And dancing like a nutter

So sad to see a dance floor
No meaning just a noise
Tripping kids off their lids
Half-naked girls and boys

Just senseless mayhem
Pointless waste of time
Young kids bouncing off their heads
Half have lost their minds

Just got to say that Marvin Gaye
Barry White as well
Beautiful music with a soulful beat
For only time will tell

Spinners, Stylistics and Supremes
Chi-Lites and many more
When the DJ puts them on

The crowd cries out for more

Hold a girl close to your chest
Feel the passion rise
Memories flood like memories do
It can even make you cry

The joy of music, the pain it brings
The summer that went so soon
And time past but played its part
Memories of a tune

I often lay awake at night
Soul music dances in my head
Not the banging type
But music that was said

Tell me that you love me
Take my pain away
Stay with me a while
Let's get on the Love Train

We are Family, Love Hurts
And also, I Will Survive
And don't forget The Bee Gees
And of course, Staying Alive

There are many DJs
Get paid for playing the crowd
But music has changed so very much
It's bangs, and played real loud

We decided to throw a party
70s is our theme
I played songs all of you know
You wondered where they've been

My music never deviated
I stayed and slowly got old
But my music that I play today
Has never ever got cold

It's hotter now than ever
People want it more
When I play Young Hearts Run Free
Everyone hits the floor

Dust off those old dancing shoes
You know it's not far away
I flew in from Los Angeles
AND ITS ME STOOD THERE AND PLAYED

# 39.    Mental Illness

She found a doorway late at night
To shelter from the storm
A coat of many colours
It helps to keep her warm

She settled down for the evening
Laughing at the rain
No one stops to help her
As she slowly goes insane

Staring at her reflection
She's found her long lost friend
They chat away the hours
Hoping night wouldn't end

Her mind is gently twisted
The forgotten left to die
Cast out on the streets of London
Her tears will make you cry

Morning broke its silence
As she bundles up her clothes
Two bags are her lifeline
As she wanders down the road

Once again, her voices
As they gather in her head
She screams for their silence
And prays they wake up dead

Alas they keep her company
And no one bares her mind

Invisible to the masses
To her they all are blind

Her plastic plate at her feet
She begs her life away
Spare a coin of fortune
Help her make it through the day

There are many just like Anne
Her scars are deep inside
She stares into another world
It's there she likes to hide

Give of your heart
Be loving and be kind
Bless these people on the street
For half have lost their mind

## 40. Alzheimer's took her Mind

Through a haze of glass
In a distant past
She reflects on dancing in the rain
She leaves behind tomorrow
But doesn't feel the pain

She brushes back her golden hair
Her mirror in a golden frame
Pictures hung with blank faces
She doesn't know their names

She holds her hands to her face
It keeps her from going insane
Music dances in her head
She laughs and never complains

The world fell all around her
Her story has no end
She left behind faded memories
Forgot the names of friends

She dreams of better days
But nothing comes to mind
Such a dreaded disease
How life can be so unkind

Late at night when darkness comes
Her shadow is by her side
She stares into a world of dreams
For there's nowhere left to hide

A field of memories lay at her feet
Like flowers in hills of grass
She tries to pick a flower
But always slips her grasp

Moments turn to years
Life has taken its toll
She tried to cope the best she can
Finally, she lost control

They walked her through the doors of life
And surrounded her with love
Comfort was the eyes of nurses
And time was not enough

They eventually laid her to rest
Placed a flower in her hands
For death finally came for her
And tomorrow is never planned

Keep your memories cherished
For today is all we have
For every fleeting moment
Are times we wished we grabbed

# 41.  Just for the Crack

Strung out from an early age
Her mother worked the streets
Tragedy from the mouths of babes
She took her whiskey neat

Late at night in the bar hall
She plied her wares for sale
Spent half her life hustling
The other half in jail

Becky was the baby
Her mother taught her well
Many days left all alone
In some seedy motel

Becky showed the bruises
From her mother's midnight slap
Turning over daytime tricks
Trying to get some crack

She packed her bags and packed some rags
Becky by her side
She robbed a man outside a store
Now she's looking for a place to hide

She turned a john for a fifty spot
Her pipe needed a glow
And demons danced inside her head
And death decided to show

She died with Becky holding her hand
And crack was the price she paid
A child's eyes became so wide

Now Becky cried her mum to the grave

The fruit fell close to a fallen tree
And crack was now Becky's date
She took over from where her mum left off
For life became her fate

And destiny plays a darkened game
A promise that has no end
And dealers dance with innocence
Pretending to be a friend

Time played a waiting game
Becky paid the price
They buried her next to her mother
And crack was her only vice

There are many Becky's
They make money on their backs
Held prisoner to a dealer
They do it Just for the Crack

# 42.    Bittersweet Morning

Bittersweet morning. I'd just like to remember all the friends we've lost throughout the years, and the tears we've shed at home and here. We can all share each other's pain. Please take a few moments while you sip your morning coffee and dance off into the sunshine to remember our friends. Often, I see Martin the plumber's smiling face walking down the road, or Nigel, or Loverman Lasky, and many, many more, not to mention mums and dads, aunties, uncles, brothers, sisters and friends that were so young and left way too early. And recently our lovely Brenda who walked the staircase to heaven. We are all one moment away from the same staircase, and life is but a fleeting moment away. So many characters that stepped into our lives and, just like snow, melted away.

I just ask you all to remember friends and relatives, and just be grateful they came into our lives. I flew home to bury my brother, who as I'm sure all readers are aware by now, was senselessly murdered in London. I say 'brother' because that's how close we were.

I want to thank my friends who donated to my brother's GoFundMe page, and I know his family and friends are really taking his death badly. Also our thoughts are with CF, who is in the UK at the moment, dealing with a family crises. So please take time out of your busy day and call a friend or family member before there is no one on the end of the line.

On a personal note, people who are in my life, thank you. I know who you are.

Love you all.

# 43.    We Age to the Grave

Born into a dream of life
A mystery to behold
Youth passes by
As slowly you become old

The bus stop shows the seated
Old with far away eyes
You pass them without a second glance
And then you realize

I too will be old and feeble
Waiting in the same line
I looked at my reflection
It's just a matter of time

My eyes are slowly fading
My hair has turned to skin
My back breaks each morning
As my day begins

My doctor is my best friend
He pumps me full of pills
He smiles when he sees me
Because he knows how I feel

The days are long behind me
The future's around the bend
So many funerals later
Saying goodbye to my friends

We gather around the grave
Staring into the hole

You ponder for a moment
Realizing you too ain't long to go

Then it's back to the grindstone
And grind your life away
Looking for some answers
It's time for you to pray

I hope I go to heaven
Maybe I'll go to hell
Is my life but a dream?
It's really hard to tell

I looked into my biscuit tin
Photos of the past
Black and white images
That went by so fast

Dad was holding an ice cream
I must have been about ten
Distant were those memories
That I'll never see again

Aunties and uncles
All have passed away
The tin that holds their memories
Of a past that didn't stay

Tragic lives that left us
And we but still remain
We dance until tomorrow
And life won't be the same

So all of us are seated
Waiting for the bus
No one leaves this world alive
We'll one day all be dust

So here is my little secret
Before you leave the stage
Dance and sing every day
Before you're aged to your grave

## 44.      Lipstick Lil

What a thrill to meet Lipstick Lil
Waiting for the train
She worked the streets of London
And her name became her fame

Her lipstick red with pleasure
Her hair the dark of night
We chatted for a while
As she asked me for a light

Her perfume filled the summer night
Her sadness she hid so well
I could see the pain of pleasure
For her body was for sale

We chatted the midnight hour
As the last train pulled to a stop
I could see the lines of sadness
For a woman time forgot

With sullen eyes and laughter
She tried to ply her wares
But time became her enemy
She just got lots of stares

My heart was broken with sadness
As she sat there all alone
I decided to show her compassion
And invite her to my home

She told me of her story
Never having a home
Her mother walked the streets at night

And left her all alone

Motels and hotels
Drugs became her best friend
Then one fateful night
Her mother's life came to an end

Fruit fell from her mother's tree
The streets became her life
Lipstick drove the men wild
And red became the night

Morning broke her silence
As Lil went on her way
I knew she had to go
But I wished that she would stay

I often think of Lipstick Lil
Waiting for the train
The sadness of a women
Who found only pain

Late one winter's night
I heard that she had died
I bowed my head into my hands
God knows that I cried

There are many Lils that walk the streets
Their stories never told
They lay their lives on the line
And sleep for the promise of gold

RIP Lipstick Lil

# 45. My son has flown the nest.

It wasn't easy letting go of my grown son. He simply walked off into the rain. And now I'm left with the same emptiness and sorrow that most dads have to endure. He's worked so hard in his chosen occupation and in Florida has found a place where he wants to live. Who could blame him? Sun, sand and sea, same as I did when I left my Mum and Dad and moved to Bournemouth.

I sit here numb and proud and hope he finds happiness and, of course, stays safe. What a few months this has been. Lost my best friend to a senseless murder, lost our lovely friend Brenda to cancer, and now my son leaves to pursue his chosen career.

The rain adds to the sadness but, as they say, life goes on. Now I know we face late nights ahead of us worrying about him and pacing the bloody floor. What are children? They are love and worry, that's what they are, from the time they're born and placed in your arms they are loved, protected and you would die for them wherever they go, worry and love and follow them. And they simply look over their shoulder, smile and leave, not understanding that they are leaving you with a broken heart.

So another chapter in the book of life comes to an end, and a new chapter starts.

This ain't pity, you know. I'm not asking for pity. This is reality of life. As you all read this, I know there are so many families suffering a million worse things. I'm just reminding all who care to read this to hold each other, or if you can't do that then just a phone call. I can't stress enough, the importance of a hug.

Holding my son, I should have done it more often. Looks like I'll be booking many trips to Florida.

# 46.   A note from Karl

*As I edit this book for the final time, wondering if we've mixed it up enough to demonstrate how the mind of someone suffering from neurosis jumps around, I've just seen my own son, Kai, off to Australia. He's got a year-long work permit, and if he does three months 'essential work' during that time it's instantly renewable for another year.*

*But supposing he doesn't ever come back then? Supposing he loves it out there, meets a girl and never comes back? Kai's my best mate. There's no one I'd rather go to the pub with than him, and I love going to boxing and football with him, especially 'away' games. He keeps me out of trouble*

*And yet three days ago – as I write – with a beautiful smile on his handsome face, his long hair and his backpack on his back he hugged me tight, told us he loves us, turned and walked away without a glance back over his shoulder.*

*Probably for the best really. He knows that. We chased him in the car, both Sue and I crying our eyes out, to get a last glimpse of him as he entered the station.*

*Don't get me wrong, we truly hope it works out for him out in Oz, and we really want him to get the best of the opportunity, but the house is so bloody empty without him.*

*So I understand Danny's sentiments above.*

# 47.  Hold time in the palm of your hand

Hold time in the palm of your hand
Count your blessings too
Life is but a piece of cake
Keep a slice for you

Show love and compassion
Don't leave it way too late
For time will pass you by
There is no time to wait

Tell people that you love them
Hold them for a while
Leave them with a tear in their eye
And leave them with a smile

I'm gonna walk into the rain today
Going to smell a flower or two
Going to laugh in the sunshine
Got so many things to do

And when my time finally comes
And my life is at an end
I shall walk the stairs to Heaven
And have a party with all my friends

Enjoy life

# 48.    Trying to get Answers

I often write about stuff in life and try to get answers but, my God, I never knew anxiety would grip me in a way that feels like I'm about to jump out of an airplane. What the hell is going on?

For those who suffer with this condition I really empathise with you. I was fine a few months ago, then out of nowhere this fear just gripped the shit out of me for no reason. Anything can trigger it. My eyesight went blurry, I'm in hospital. I had a headache, I'm in hospital. My veins on the back of my hands swelled up due to a trapped nerve, and I'm back in hospital.

The mornings are the worst. This gut-wrenching fear that waits to mess with me. I'm healthy as a horse, yet the worry kicks in. What the fuck is all that about?

I know I'm dealing with the death of my best friend in the UK and the fear of what awaits me. And of course, saying goodbye to my lovely Brenda, Wolfie and Perry. I went to see our friend dealing with cancer and that also triggered a fear that really frightened the life out me. And watching my son leave home also added to the stress.

I can't imagine the rest of my friends out there who must also be dealing with this condition. My doctor said its common. I really am at a loss to know what a lot of people are going through. My sister-in-law, Rita, for example; what a fighter, always a smile. She has down days of course, but when I think of this I should be ashamed to have anxiety, but if you've never experienced it, it's hard to describe. I read about children dying and parents dealing with that. Also a personal friend whose son got shot, and they have to deal with helping him regain the use of his legs.

My heart breaks for you all. I can't understand where you find the strength. I'm so guilt-ridden that I'm ashamed because, as I say, I have everything; I'm healthy, I have a beautiful wife and the world is at my feet. I want friends to let me know what the secret is. The secret to day-to-day life. My daughter has been dealing with it all her life, and now I'm searching for answers from her. It must run in the family. I truly hope anyone who reads this book contacts me, opens up and talks to me.

I used to be the class clown, but this condition has wiped the makeup off my face. If anyone out there is in the same boat as me, drop me a line and talk about it. Please don't hide away. I would love to chat with you. You'll find me on Facebook. Inbox me and I'll help you as much as you can help me

Love ya

## 49.  When Anxiety Attacks

Good morning heart, how are you?
It's the calm before the storm
I'm fine, my love, but there's a pain
Up and down my arm

Maybe you're having a heart attack
Are you sure that you're okay?
I'm starting to beat a little faster
The ambulance is on its way

My world passes like a fireball
My brain is racing too
My lungs feel like they're dying
All you hear is code blue

Wires, nurses and doctors
Machines that make a beep
They strap you on the gurney
And talk to you so sweet

A calming voice is all you need
Reassuring doctor's words
A bedside manner well-rehearsed
This anxiety is a curse

Back home to my four walls
The cycle is about to begin
The demons start to knock on the door
But I dare not let them in

Screams that no one hears
And no one understands

The fear that breaks my soul
No matter how strong I am

It builds and builds like pressure
I wait for it to explode
My brain starts to mess with me
Says, So soon you will be old

Then in comes anxiety and panic
Who the fuck let them in?
I was doing great this week
It's a battle I have to win

Anxiety took the first swing
I ducked and hit the floor
Panic punched me in my gut
I said, I ain't taking this no more

I stood and faced my demons
I bit off both their heads
I'm doing better day-by-day
It's harder than I said

So those of you who suffer
Don't hide the fear that pain
You're just like most of us
And you're not going insane

It's a chemical imbalance
There's no magic cream to rub
You have to be tough and strong
And welcome to the club

# 50.    After Seeking Medical Advice

So, after seeking medical advice, and $250 dollars lighter, talking to a specialist revealed that "The truth to life is in your hands."

It's a road we all walk down and have to pick ourselves up. Life is not easy, even with money, no one is truly happy. This therapist was more interested in my accent, and so we focused on the UK. I explained my situation, with the passing of my friend, and she said that I talk too much, which is hiding my emotion. I told her this is my normal personality.

Anyway, she found the root of my trouble, which is I never grieved when my parents died. I held it in. Anxiety needs to feed on a problem. It will eat you alive. She was a lovely lady, she was even overcome by my parent's passing. I explained I had to fly home every month. Most of us ex-pats lose parents and the grief is held in because we live in America. We think they're still alive at home and that's how we deal with it. Does that make sense?

You must remember that we're all living 6000 miles from home and we have all left behind memories and families. We have all sacrificed a lot just to find happiness in the sun. Anxiety is very common, hence the number of drugs that are taken by 10.5 million people who are currently on Xanax. We all face tragedy and that's the fact of life, simple. You must wait your turn and wait for the dreaded phone call

The truth is that life is bittersweet. Sometimes it's beautiful. I see family photos on Facebook, mums and dads and families and friends enjoying California from the UK, but as time goes by those photos fade and all that's left are memories.

We are all photographs, and we all stay in the moment and embrace each other. We are ALL a moment away from anxiety. There is a cure and it's simple. Talk.

Talk, chat, go for coffee with a real friend, reach out, call someone. We are all so wrapped up in our own world. Pick up the bloody phone. That's what anxiety hates, that you are ignoring her. Go for a walk, listen to music, dance, sing and stop the madness. Read a book even. Read one of my friend Karl's books. I promise he'll make you laugh. He writes the funniest books. Just search Karl Wiggins on Amazon, and I promise you'll cry laughing

Let me tell you something; I was always the comedian, I made everyone laugh, but what a lot of people don't know is that someone has to make the comic laugh. And Karl was the one to make me laugh. Try his books. I promise you'll laugh out loud

When we all moved out to California in the 1980's, Karl stayed three years and then moved on along what he terms as pre-destined paths. He had other lives to live, which was great. But what wasn't so great was that we lost touch. I'll never forgive myself for that. But when I found him again after all these years, I wrote to him and said;

"Karl, it's been a very long time since you stepped into my world and made me laugh. I don't think I could have survived in Bournemouth without your company, and now I find you writing books and still making people laugh. Oh my GOD, Karl, you were the funniest lad I could have roomed with at the Palace Court. You really MUST write about those days! I never had a brother and I think you filled those shoes, if only for a moment. So happy to see your smiling face again on your profile photo. I don't think I ever saw you sad. Anyway Mr Wiggins, just wanted you to know that there will always be a special part in my heart that will be forever grateful for your friendship. We had some laughs eh? Stay well young lion, I can't wait to read your books, Danny."

Taste Karl's books. Search Karl Wiggins on Amazon, and I promise you'll cry laughing.

## 51.     We are All Just Pictures

Everyone has pictures
We put them into frames
Their blank faces stare out
Some are forgotten names

Albums of memories
Many passed away
A moment captured
On some sunny day

Uncle Fred and Auntie Pam
Twilight, romance and years
Distance time in war torn life
Black and white and tears

The creased and torn photos
In a biscuit tin of life
Those wedding scenes of long-gone years
Some stranger and his wife

Babies turn to ladies
Children now all grown
And granddad Charlie fell asleep
So sad he died alone

We are all just photographs
A glimpse in someone's book
A face you knew so long ago
You take a second look

Was that Uncle Albert
So young and in his prime

He lived to be eighty-five
Then eventually ran out of time

Everyone's a picture
A frameless work of the heart
A silent voice upon the wall
Some say they call it art

I am but a picture
Caught up in my prime
A frame that hangs me on a wall
My face, it's just a matter of time

Roses and flower crosses
A grave that holds a wreath
Mourners with umbrellas
Dealing with their grief

They say time is but a healer
Everything will be okay
And staring into sullen eyes
That's all you think to say

A shoulder tries to help in vain
A kiss to ease the heart
But silence steals the moment
For love that's torn apart

Words are broken like shards of glass
Nothing fills the abyss
Rage and anger fill the void
Of the love that will surely be missed

Screams and heartfelt pain
Voices that mute the tongue
Senseless act of violence
To be taken way too young

And so we gather voices
To comfort a broken heart
Alas for words fall silent
Not knowing where to start

Grief holds no prisoners
It's cold with deep revenge
It knows no love or sympathy
Only you can make it end

Try to remember the good times
Beat grief at its own game
If you feel sadness brewing
Try to swallow your pain

Walk where there are rainbows
Laugh in the pouring rain
Hold your head high in the sky
Let grief feel your pain

There are no secrets to life
There is something you can do
If you want to beat grief
I'm afraid it's up to you

Throw your shoulders back
Face the mighty foe
I know its early days
Take it very slow

We shall all be a mighty tree
We are all of the same leaf
And when the storm comes
We shall all share the same grief

## 52.    Half Empty or Half Full

You either look at life half empty or half full. I love life and people, even the ones I know who don't like me because, who knows, maybe they think I'm trying to be flash, but I'm not. This truly is my personality.

And for those who don't like it, I'll let you into a secret. I sleep naked just in case you want to kiss my ass!

You see, I was born blessed, and I've never changed my personality. I can't help it.

Love yourself. I know it's hard at times, trust me, I know it's hard, but this book is not for people dealing with real tragedy. This book is for those, like me, that need a kick up arse. Those who are healthy and can get on a bike and enjoy life.

I've seen tragedy close up, and I'm here to tell about my own psychic tension. My friends, we can beat this

Love ya and I repeat what I keep saying throughout this book. I'm here anytime for a chat. Anytime

## 53.    And Laughter

And laughter. Laughter is often your only real defence. You know what laughter is? It's you standing proud and saying, "Not today, mate, not today. Today you can fuck off. I've survived everything the world's thrown at me up to this point. And so today I'm going to laugh."

## 54.    I slept with Miss Anxiety

Went to bed with Anxiety
She kept me up all night
She crawled into my heart
And squeezed it real tight

Come on let's dance
As I tried to catch my breath
She squeezed a little tighter
As my heart burst out my chest

She sang and played a set of drums
Then Panic came through the door
I tried to calm her down
But she wanted to dance some more

Panic threw a hissy fit

And said that's not fair
Open up the windows
Let's bring in some air

Mr Calm was full of charm
As he took the drums away
He brought in Miss Xanax
And she told them they couldn't stay

Finally got a little sleep
Knowing Anxiety is at my door
She keeps on pacing and
Walking up and down the floor

I installed a peep hole
Got Miss Xanax to keep an eye
If I hear her knocking
Just let her walk on by

And those of you who know Anxiety
Here's what you should do
Don't let her in your head
Keep Panic away too

Just grab a piece of sunshine
Grab a piece of cake
If you invite Anxiety in
You're making a big mistake

Go and ride a bicycle
Try not to stay at home
Anxiety loves to visit you
When you're all alone

She hates when you ignore her
Eventually she'll go away
But if you offer her attention

That bitch will want to stay

So this is the story
Of Panic and stress
Anxiety is the leader
And will lead you to distress

So gather friends around you
Pick up your phone
Try your best in every way
Not to be alone

I'm here if you need me
Just call out my name
And if i need you
I will do the same

RIP Anxiety, Panic & Stress

## 55.    Skin Cancer

I'm often accused of writing about depressing subjects, so please, if this bothers you, then you really should have swerved this book. Don't read my drivel. It's the way I deal with my demons

I've never hidden from ridicule.

Then, on the other hand, I do read other people's drivel.

I'm always on top of my skin. Twenty-eight minor ops and counting. They're not really serious, although melanoma certainly can be. I've had sarcoma and basal cell carcinoma. The term skin cancer is also thrown around by the dermatologist to frighten you. I wrote a depressing cancer poem and I got a lot of flak for it, so I've decided not to include it here.

It was shit anyway.

I wrote it to warn people to never leave it too late. What's wrong with shedding light on a taboo subject?

My heart goes out to all those who are suffering.

## 56.   Drink Found Me

Gin and tonic, vodka dry
Brandy nice and sweet
Drink my bourbon just like wine
Take my whisky neat

Olive for my troubles
Cherry to dress my taste
Ice to cool those summer nights
Let nothing go to waste

My lips hang with pleasure
As I sip my life away
Temptation plays her part so well
It's a price I have to pay

One more for the road
Two more for a laugh
Fill my dreams to the top
Never take my glass

Morning wakes me early
A cigarette for my chest
Battle scars face me
Let the bottle do the rest

A lonely stool of solitude
A bartender with a smile
A sarcastic sneer of gratitude
Haven't seen you in a while

The darkness of a sunken soul
The bitter taste of sin

He pours my troubles in a glass
As my day begins

In walks little Daisy
Carrying her life in a bag
She sits alone in the corner
It makes me feel so sad

She stares off into a better place
And stirs her dreams away
Loneliness found her long ago
And decided he would stay

Burt the bullshit artist
A story for every ear
Politeness is not my strongest point
So I made my point real clear

Tommy's in the wide-awake club
His son got killed in the war
He looks around for company
I don't think he can take anymore

He drowns his sorrow in vodka
Stirred with a touch of class
And tears add to the mixture
As he looks down in his glass

A room falls silent to pleasure
They all stare down at their drink
A businessman in a shirt and tie
Said drink helps him think

The jukebox plays Patsy Cline
The bartender's favourite song
He cleans his glasses very well
And also sings along

It's time for me to stagger home
Pissed my life down the drain
When morning finds me half-asleep
It will find me down the pub again

I don't know why I wrote that. I don't even drink.

## 57.  Why did Danny write that poem (by Karl)

Well, I guess, it's his way of showing understanding for those who use alcohol, or drugs even, to push their anguish to the back of their minds. To bury it.

The same reason he writes about prostitution I suppose and the connection between that and drug abuse.

The trouble with burying your anguish, though, is that everything they're trying to bury, all their low spirits and despair and despondency and anguish and heartache are like letters posted through a letter-box that they're not picking up, and the pile of letters is getting bigger and bigger and bigger until one day they're going to trip over them and come crashing down.

You can't bury heartache. You can't "get over it." It's like a ball at the beach. No matter how many times you try and push it under the water it just comes bouncing back up again, sometimes in front of you, and sometimes behind you. But at the wrong time and in the wrong place. You just snap!

And who knows what happens then?

*Why do you snap? Because it's all bubbling away beneath the surface of your psyche. It's part of your élan vital, but you bury it by snorting the answer up your nose or slurping down alcohol and everything's great again. Except it isn't great, is it?*

*Anguish and heartache and despair shouldn't be entombed. They have to be addressed to give yourself closure.*

*Easier said than done, though, I know, but alcohol's not the answer*

## 58.    Time to Go

I packed my bags this morning
Black suit and my tie
My plane sits on the tarmac
It's time for me to fly

The anguish of this moment
Death has taken its toll
It's only a matter of time now
I'm afraid I have to go

The silence of the morning
The bitter taste of tears
Reflecting on a life gone by
Embracing all those years

Looking for my passport
As the world just passes by
No one sees the pain I'm in
Except the tears I cry

Catch me if I fall
Hold me for a while
I played my part so very well
Hiding behind my smile

Ten long hours awaits me
Seats that all recline
Gazing out into the abyss
Counting down the time

Gentle fake faces
Asking me for a drink

Caught up in the moment
Having plenty of time to think

May I have glass of wine
She smiles as she was trained
She brings me red instead of white
Can't be bothered to complain

I hear the captain's voice
I have waited for so long
We land in fifteen minutes
I know I must be strong

Welcome to Great Britain
It's not a welcome for me
I'm going to bury my best friend
It's time to let him be

The bitterness of the weather
The gentle taste of rain
The only wish I have
Is I shall see my brother again

Let me say to all of you
That this is not the end
Just mention him from time to time
From Danny, your best friend

## 59.    Kiss Me Goodbye

Tears fail my broken heart
Words are not enough
'Tis now I bleed deep inside
Didn't know life would be this tough

Sweet summer sadness
Bitter taste of rain
My heart aches deep inside
Silence is my pain

And now I face tomorrow
Envy of my youth
To see my past behind me
And help me face the truth

I shall sleep in restless slumber
Awakened by the dawn
Kiss the sky above me
Thankful for being born

I can see heavens above me
I know they wait with time
Let me kiss my friend goodbye
The love I lost was mine

So I'll wait with open arms
Until my days to come
And in your arms I won't walk to you
For in your arms I'll run

## 60.    Miss You, My Wonderful Friend

Not even time can heal me
Since you went away
Lost my world to madness
There are only words to say

Broken and my memories
I'm a shadow of a man
I lost the will to carry on
Catch me if you can

I have fallen into an endless pit
With the whisper of your name
Alone in this dreaded world
Nothing remains the same

Pictures tell your story
The kindness and your heart
Days pass over my shoulder
My world has been torn apart

I see your face in a reflection
Alas it's my mistake
I don't know how much more
My broken heart can take

Music takes me back
When all of us were young
So sad you were taken way too soon
Your life had just begun

Late at night I dance with shadows
You stepped into my dreams

I try so hard to carry on
It's harder than it seems

I speak to Dave who sends his love
His heart is broken too
We carry on day by day
All we talk about is you

Sharon misses you so very much
She tries to carry on
We all help her as much as we can
And help her to stay strong

I stay in touch with Joel and Paul
Their life is not the same
They're both lost in agony
They're all feeling the pain

So goodnight my sweet prince
Until we meet again
We all miss and love you
From all of your friends

# 61.    My old home gone

They pulled our church down
At the end of my road
Now the faithful
Have nowhere to go

The graves remain silent
Just names etched in stone
And flowers keep them company
Better than being alone

The past keeps her vigil
With the passing of time
My childhood memories
Are all in my mind

Rain adds to the sadness
On a cold winters' day
The park is closed now
Where I used to play

My childhood innocence
And my boyish smile
I look over my shoulder
It's been quite a while

I can still see young faces
Walking to school
The gates are all gone now
And so is the wall

Umbrella and buses
With traffic and rain
Old sullen smiles

While hiding their pain

And there sits an old lady
With far away eyes
We chatted a while
She said everything dies

She shuffled away with
Two bags by her side
The streets are her home now
And that's where she'll die

I leave in the morning
On the first early flight
For those too who are leaving
Please turn off the light

# 62.    I Stand

One of the hardest things for me was to speak at my best friend's funeral, which is why I had to ask for help before my emotions brought me to my knees. We all stood united with his wife and his family and friends. I wanted to celebrate his life, not his death. I have always loved the quote 'Kiss the Sky.' I will be forever kissing the sky. I wrote this poem which I feel sums up my love for him. I cherish our 42 years of friendship. Wait for me as we must wait for you.

I stand before you a broken man
My best friend has just died
A senseless act of violence
No chance to say goodbye

I stand with a broken heart
Memories fall like rain
Those boyish smiles we shared
Have now all turned to pain

I stand and try to understand
I sleep every once in a while
All the time I think of him
And seeing his wonderful smile

I stand with all of you
Embrace the love we've lost
We walk a road paved with pain

This tragedy and loss

Please everyone stand with me
Join me in applause
Let God welcome him home
Let Angels open the doors

Let not grief hold your heart
But memories of the past
Remember him as he was
His kindness and his heart

I stand beside you
Dave, I'm by your side
Lorraine and Paul, I'm over your shoulder
To catch the tears you cried

So I ask all of you
Please stand and be brave
I shall be with all of you
As we stand around my best friend's grave


RIP, my best friend, taken too soon. Love ya, wait for me as I must wait for you.

# 63.     Leaving the UK after the Funeral

No wonder people take Xanax. The world is fucking cruel. Perhaps it's all part of God's plan, and (as my friend Karl would say) part of our Earthwalk is to learn compassion.

Now our lovey Shaun has died, and my auntie has passed on. Everywhere there is grief. There are no answers to the suffering and to watch my friend in agony is heart wrenching. There are no words to help, nothing you can do or say that can turn the clock back, so for all my family and friends, Christmas and the New Year wasn't the same. But we all had to carry on!

Once again, I want to offer support for all who are dealing with grief and tragedy. If you are suffering and need help, see your doctor and *take back* your life as opposed to *taking* your life!

The pressure to deal with life is very stressful, but there is help out there.

Never did I think that stress would knock on my door. Worrying about bills, and friends crossing over can really play havoc on your brain. So, a big hug to all of you. Take one day at a time. You can't change what you can't control, but you can get back to controlling your life. Don't feed into grief. Take one day, one second at a time. I can't promise that everything will be okay, that's entirely up to you. But just remember, your heart and mind can pull you out of dark places. You only have to reach out and friends will be there. And if you feel you have no one, I'll be there for you. I'll be only too happy to chat.

Love you all.

I really need a hug.

*A hug, an embrace, is really so undervalued, notably those hugs that are so close and snug that you can actually taste the other person's lifeforce, and you've never felt so secure*

*Hug someone special.*

## 64.    Back to the Grindstone

Ten-day trip to bury my best friend, but he's still alive. He lives in me.

And then it was back to grindstone of life leaving behind Mum, Dad, Aunties, Uncles, Friends, and I felt guilty that I'm still able to function.

I walked around gravestones and read names etched in slabs of polished granite, and the rain just added to the fucking sadness of it all! How can you not be moved by the silence of graves? I get it, trust me, I get it. Holding my stupid jokes inside my head and biting my tongue. I wanted to fucking scream and shout and say 'enough is enough' but death just keeps on rolling out the red carpet. My good mate, Alfie, summed it up, 'Danny, we're not twenty anymore, mate.' That really shook me! And now I'm off to say goodbye to Shaun, a lad whose laughter would melt your heart. A gentle soul who died of cancer so young.

God seems to be getting blamed for all the deaths, and I have no answers except to somewhat agree with my friend, Karl, who tells me they're simply needed elsewhere in the universe.

Life is but a bus ride, and some step off way too early.

So again, I say to all of you, taste the rain, kiss the sky, walk in sunshine, talk to your kids, love your family, call them on the phone and make sure you tell all of them you love them. You might as well get kissed to death

I don't have the answer to life. I've got no answers at all. I'm just lucky to have a front row ticket to the greatest show on earth.

Out of all the trillions and trillions and trillions of humans that have graced this planet, we were born for a purpose. What that is, who knows? But I'm sure it's all about learning lessons and supporting each other.

## 65.    Solitude in my Brain

Don't expect you to understand
Unless you're in my head
I worry about my actions
Or the stupid things I've said

A wheel that keeps on turning
Never finding peace
Hide my feelings deep inside
But wear my heart upon my sleeve

You hope to find some answers
Praying for some help
The therapist knows nothing
And she just helps herself

Rain that plays her part so well
Another dreadful day
We all gather round the table
Wondering what to say

The noise of silence in my head
The solitude of my mind
All my friends lost so soon
They simply ran out of time

Life with all its trimmings
A plate that overflows
And in my head is sadness
But no one really knows

The clown wipes off his makeup
The distance of the past

I dance around inside my head
I'm finally home at last

Loneliness finds me
It whispers in my head
You can rest a while
As I lay back in my bed

Darkness in a naked brain
Stripped down to the bone
Slumber keeps me company
Better than being alone

A gentle kiss is all I ask
Arms that could melt snow
Alas I awake everyday
And once again alone

Some say I'm funny
Many say I'm insane
Just hold me for one moment
So there's no solitude in my brain.

# 66.    Cry into the Moon

I leave behind my memories
My tears I keep inside
My heart will always be with you
My arms are open wide

It's only a phone call
I'm just a letter away
If I'm ever needed
I can be with you in a day

Don't cry for me Auntie Christine
My path leads me home
I shall leave the door open
In case you're ever alone

I danced and laughed my youth away
You were always by my side
And now I must dance to a different tune
The pain is so hard to hide

When summer comes to Scotland
And the hills will call you home
We shall be waiting at the airport
No more tears on the phone

My silver birds waits for me
Her wings will fly so soon
I love you Auntie Christine
Watch me cry into the moon

## 67.     Peter Pan Will Eventually Die

I was in bits at Chalkie's funeral. Such a savage, unnecessary, brutal killing. And such a cowardly attack. I know what it takes to be mentally strong. I am weak and need help, but because I'm always funny I'm not supposed to be weak or need help. I hide all my problems behind my jokes. Behind my smile is a world of misery. The thing is nobody really knows if someone's bruised inside, or what it took to drag their arse out of bed and look presentable enough to face the day. You could be sitting next to someone on the bus who is absolutely destroyed, and you'd never know it. Especially when they hide behind their stupid jokes.

Friends, sometimes I laugh so no one can hear me scream!

It's killing me day by day. It chips away at your soul. It breaks you. It's relentless. And it's a circle. You wake up one morning with a little bit of blurred vision, and your brain says you have a tumour, so you're back in hospital, tests all negative, but your brain says they might have missed something. Then you're up all bloody night worrying about death and getting old. Then the fear wants to join in, then the sweats, then all hell breaks loose, and you want to end the suffering so you start planning your suicide.

I'm not going to top myself, it's just a cry for help. It's all to do with stress, anxiety, worry and falling into a black pit of depression. The end is close, so that's it really. Peter Pan will eventually die, that is the simple truth.  No psycho doctor can turn the clock back. We die. That's it in a nutshell. And I'm the fucking nutcase in the shell!

But life goes on and having the coffin of your best friend on your shoulder doesn't help

I want to know the secret of old people, old people who ain't got long, dancing and singing. How do they fucking do that? That's what I want. I want to be able to do that.

## 68.    Children Grown and Gone

Their rooms are a reminder
The memories of their youth
Children's lies and laughter
No one telling the truth

Now there's just emptiness
A mother's silent tear
She reflects with fondness
On all her children's years

The many nights of baby's cries
Chasing room to room
How quickly time passes
They have left so soon

Birds fly the coup of life
A nest that breaks your heart
For now they fly so high
Their lives about to start

Our phones will be our lifeline
The updates of their life
The worry of the distance
When the phone call comes at night

And as I pass their bedroom
I can still hear those running feet
And beds that still remind us
When our kids were fast asleep

So we shall grow old and weary
Our children still young with youth
I shall always remember the good times
When we all lived under the same roof

# 69.    We Are All Time Bombs

So, turning 60 has really put a dent in my armour of life, and obviously this poor old heart is still pounding away, thank God. Many who have been lucky enough to go unscathed; well done. Or perhaps I should say thank your genes. However, too much food and alcohol and fast food really add up. We should all consider the downfall and shortness of life when choosing fatty foods and alcohol and smoking etc.

The body is an amazing machine and we all take it for granted. I want to bring a little wakeup call in here and, without standing on a bloody soap box, I just want you to take care of yourselves. I know many friends who have had a stent in their heart to keep any blocked passages open, and life is great. But - and listen GOOD - the stent only lasts ten years. Studies show that the stent itself can become blocked. Plaque collects more on the wall of the stent than the wall of the artery. Listen to your body. Shortness of breath, indigestion, pain, if your jaw is numb, or your left arm, a cardiogram is the only good way to check your heart. But a nuclear stress test is the only way to really see if you have a blockage.

Basically, they inject a dye called radionuclide, which lights up and circulates through your blood stream. They then use a gamma camera to take pictures of your heart, and that'll tell if you have any blocked or partially blocked arteries. Well, it won't tell *you*, because you don't know what the fuck you're looking at, but it'll tell the old ticker doctor, and he's generally pretty clued-up. They call these blockages 'cold spots,' and they indicate that your heart muscles aren't getting enough blood during exercise.

The thing is, the insurance company does not like to spend money and will simply fob you off with a cheaper test. They'd rather you die than have to spend money. Please, please INSIST on a nuclear stress test. We are all time bombs walking around.

In fact, don't wait for any symptoms to show up. Get a five-year check-up, even if you haven't had the stent installed.

So that's it from Doctor Dan. You can take care of yourself, or take my advice with a pinch of salt, but trust me, any blockage in your heart will cause you real problems. We're all getting older now, so I urge you all DON'T, DON'T see your doctor. Your doctor will only say, "You're fine, fuck off."

You must see a cardiologist.

And here's the strangest thing, my cardiology doctor trained under my Mum's heart doctor in the UK. Small world, eh?

Your heart is in your hands. Take care of yourselves. No one else will.

# 70.     He Froze in Birmingham

The streets were littered with bodies
Winter storm came in
Many huddled in doorways
Others found homes in bins.

Cardboard was his mattress
Paper wrapped his feet
Covered with an old overcoat
There he fell asleep.

His company was a bottle
He drank to hide his pain
The morning broke with a whisper
He died in the freezing rain.

There he lied and fell asleep
In his ragged clothes
The winter storm came at night
This was how he froze.

No one came to see him
There he died alone
All he needed was a shelter
A shelter he could call home.

Many face the same fate
Their story should be told
We need to help the homeless
And get them out of the cold.

If you have a blanket
Or a coat that you can spare

Give to a homeless person
Tell them that you care.

If you see them hungry
Spare a little bread
Don't wait until it's too late
For you may find them dead.


This concerns a homeless man discovered dead on the streets of Birmingham, West Midlands, UK. CCTV footage shows another man searching through his pockets as he slumps against a wall. A man behind is getting ready to inject himself and another man drinks from a can of beer. According to witnesses, the body lay at the scene for five hours before the authorities were called.

## 71.    Christmas in a Homeless Heart

Snow fell on Christmas Day
The gift they got was cold
They huddled in the doorway of life
The young and the very old

Strung out and abandoned
Left out in the snow
No shelter to lay their heads
Nowhere else to go

Thrown out like garbage
The smell evokes the same
People pass them by
Even in the rain

Some with yesterday's paper
A pillow for their head
Life offers no lifeline
Many wash up dead

No funeral, just a footprint
Just a memory in the sand
A lonely old lady
Life was not as she planned

She sits with a bonnet
And lays it at her feet
Ask to spare a copper
To get her something to eat

That's where they found her
Her bonnet by her side
No one came to see her
On the day she died

Only tears of rain
Washed away her soul
Once again death came early
For there's nowhere for her to go

Night-time in the doorway
The cold cut their breath
Life on the streets
And the promise of death

When you're warm
In the comfort of your home
Break a little bread
For the ones on their own

For the cold and the tired
The lame and the weak
Give thought to others
Who are sleeping on the streets

But for the grace of God
My plate of life is full
Only a moment away
Tragedy can happen to you

There's only Christmas in a homeless heart
The cold to keep them warm
And life played out its part so well
On the day that you were born

Gather round the table of life
Thank God you've somewhere to go
Life can throw you out on the streets
Now you're the one in the Snow
Merry Christmas to the homeless

# 72.    Christmas 2018

I'm a bit emotional. My best friend has left us way too soon, and I'm sick and tired of sadness and death, of friends we won't see anymore. For those who know me it's been the worst year of my life, and I'm hoping that with your help we can all get together and embrace each other. That's the best gift you can give me.

I'm sending love to my friends; Sharon, Dave and Lorraine, and their families in the UK. Here's a small poem to soak you all in love.

### Time is but our enemy

Don't come to my funeral
I won't be there
Don't tell me you love me
I won't be able to care

Don't bring me flowers
Or tell me I'm great
Tell me now that you love me
Don't make me wait

I can't hear your voices
I can't see your pain
I am gone forever

And won't be back again

Your words, they are silent
Your kisses are gone
I can't hear the music
In my favourite song

Fill my heart with joy
But don't fill the seats
Hold me now
And kiss my cheeks

Don't speak in a whisper
But shout from your heart
Tell me you love me
Before we're apart

My grave awaits
My time is unknown
Don't come to my funeral
Come to my home

Knock on my door
With a big embrace
Tell me you love me
And do it to my face

And when I'm gone
There's no need to cry
Speak to me now
Before I die

No need for flowers
Call me on the phone
Do it now
Before I am gone

# 73. Another Christmas under Santa's Belt

I couldn't wait to get 2018 bloody gone. It was a hell of a year, back home in the UK as well as here in California. The palm trees and the sun can't help ease the pain. My friends and family have taken a kicking, and I can't find the words to ease their pain. Grief has really come to town. No Christmas presents can replace the heartache that I've witnessed. So for them it wasn't a Merry Christmas or a Happy New Year. I wish I had a magic wand that could help all my friends.

'Brother wind and sister rain
Cleanse my heart from grief and pain'

That's Gypsy sorcery by the way. I didn't write it. A lot of Gypsy sorcery is rooted not simply in folklore, but in tradition, passed on to us from the past. Kind of ghostly once you realise that our ancestors are still teaching us today. Gypsy beliefs kind of roll around the idea of infusing Christian thought with Pagan religions. That's the crux of the Gypsy soul.

My lovely brother sleeps in eternal bliss, along with many of my cousins in the UK. What a year 2018 was! I'm sure most people who read these words are dealing with grief in one way or another, and I'm not surprised we're all on Xanax or Trazodone or Venlafaxine or Diazepam or

Valium or Alprazolam or Lorazepam or Librium or Prozac! GET OFF THE FUCKING SWEETS, DANNY!

I truly wish you all comfort in recognition of your loss. You're not alone and, as they say, the show must go on. We just carry on and try to be normal.

I'd like to take the opportunity here to thank all my friends for all your concerns about my mental health. I'm okay. Since opening up about anxiety I have been surprised to discover the number of people who have suffered in silence. I opened the door and people stuck their heads in for a chat. And it turns out they too are dealing with it.

I was DJing the other night and one of my friends, who shall remain private, was chatting to me, when he told me he too is dealing with anxiety and psychic tension. We're going for a coffee, I hope, and a chat. That's the best Christmas gift you can give each other, and that is the gift of yourself. The greatest gift in life is companionship.

So to all who read this book, I pray you find happiness and peace. I truly hope you can laugh at the confusion.

Everything happens for a reason.

## 74.    New Year 2018/2019 (by Karl)

*I hope 2018 was good to all who read this. It was an up and down year for us. How can I list my personal events?*

- *Great holiday in the Algarve, where we celebrated our 25th Wedding Anniversary with a dinner for 12 people. Our son, Kai, flew over to join us and took care of the bill for me, so no one would see me sneaking up to pay. He also gave a speech for us that night*
- *While we were in Portugal we heard that our friend, Chalkie, had been fatally stabbed. That hit us hard. You don't expect that to happen. If you'd read about it in the papers you'd have naturally assumed it was drugs or gang-related, but he just went out to do a day's work as a plumber, and was murdered in the most savage way possible.*
- *That affected a lot of us pretty hard, because he was a lovely guy. The police kept his body for over two months*
- *Upon return from holiday, and following a two-day rest, I wrote my car off on the way to work. Again, I won't go into details but I*

was out of it (medically not through alcohol or drugs). Most people have nightmares when they're asleep. Not me, I woke up INTO a nightmare. I'd written my car off, plus smashed two other cars up, but I was relatively unharmed. I guess someone was looking out for me because I was going about 25mph. Five minutes later I'd have been on the A41 doing 70mph.

- They let me out of hospital that day. I don't remember much about it but I 'floated' for two days. It honestly felt as if some kind of a Life Force was leaving me. For two whole days I floated between life and death.

- I lost all my confidence. I went out for a drink with our son, Kai. Someone spoke to us. I replied and then asked Kai, "Was that alright? Was I okay? Did I sound normal?" Kai assured me I was fine, and that I was making too much of it

- And then another tragedy hit, and my wife, Sue, had to leave for eight days, and I was left on my own, having smashed up my car five days earlier, and still not in the land of the living

- I was terrified. Every night I was afraid. Everyone was dying around me and I thought 'they' were coming for me next, whoever 'they' are, and there was no way I was going without a fight. I've never been so scared.

- During the daytime we had builders in the house and I didn't have the strength to argue with them. I hated them. During the day I'd walk the dog and hate them, and at night I'd be all anxious and spooked

- Sue and Kai were gone for eight days, and I counted the nights. When they returned I was so relieved to have life back in the house again
- Gradually I recovered my confidence and returned to work
- The police finally released Chalkie's body. His funeral was in Bournemouth in November. A year earlier in Bournemouth, 92 of us met for a reunion from the late 70's and early 80's when we were all carefree scamps, getting up to mischief. Danny flew over from California to DJ, as he had done a few months earlier for a party in Essex. But this time we met for a much sadder reason.
- And then it was Christmas. The three of us went to the Madness Christmas Concert at the O2, which is always a good concert. Kai and I went to the O2 again for the Whyte/Chisora fight - their first fight was tremendous. We've become solid fight fans. We were at Wembley to see Joshua's last fight, although I won't go to Wembley again for boxing. It's too big. And there are too many tourists. Not real fight fans
- And now we await the court case. I hope this cunt goes down for life, plus 100 years IPP

*All in all, a bad few months that tested our strength, and our solidarity, but we're still standing, aren't we?*

# 75.    New Year 2018/2019 by Danny

I defy anyone to have a coffin on their shoulder, bury their best friend, fly back to Los Angeles and stay normal. You'd have to be made of stone. Yet I'm told by my therapist that it's part of life and is to be expected. That tragedy befalls many people and families.

Is that supposed to make me feel better!

So if I seem angry with 2018, yes I am! 2018 can fuck off real fast. The future lies with my son, who is in Florida, making the world a safer place, and my daughter, who is in Ireland finding happiness. My gorgeous wife is ready to party, and my job is to cheer everyone up with music. So please forgive me if I seem a little out of step, but my bloody legs are buckling under the pressure of grief. I really am trying to put one step in front of the other and it's only my friends who keep me going. Thank you.

# 76. How can I Trust the Doctor?

I feel a lot better now, but the worry that they might have missed something never goes away. I imagine the worst, and the slightest concerns send my brain racing. I have to be reassured time and time again. I know I'm okay. It's very frustrating, but I can't help my thoughts. It's a living hell. Even if I have a small problem I fixate on it and the fear is overwhelming. It's very common apparently. I'm told I have an OCD condition. I fucking lose track of them all. I don't think there's anything left I haven't got!

You see, once I get told by a specialist that any type of results are negative I go to another doctor to get it confirmed. And then I go to another one. I'm always thinking, "What else could this illness be? Have I been misdiagnosed? Did the doctor fail to diagnose me?" I hear the frequency of missed or misdiagnosis is way too high. How exactly did the doctor figure it out? How does his thought process work? Is he like a kind of detective? I fucking hope so. Has he got a list of all the possible diagnoses that could explain what is medically wrong with me? And does he start narrowing down the process by finding clues that don't fit? Or does he rush through it because it's Friday and he wants to get off to see his mistress. Is that where his head's at? Thinking about the nurse he's shagging?

What about me?

I don't mean is he thinking about shagging me, although he might be. Supposing he's thinking about shagging me instead of concentrating on my diagnosis? Fuck him. I'm going to get someone else. How can I trust this prick!

# 77. Just when you think you're all good and healthy

Let me give you an example, through the eyes of an anxiety brain;

You get a sniffly nose, then along comes a cough, just a tickle at first. A week goes by, you're coughing more and more and you feel like shit, and you're also coughing up a fucking lung.

So you brave work and by the time three weeks have gone by it's worse and not shifting. Now you're dying, and I mean dying. So off to the doctor who, by the way, is sick of looking at me. Same old procedure, antibiotics and bed. NOT WORKING and bills have to be paid. So four weeks into hell and I get pneumonia. Can't pneumonia kill you? I read somewhere that the mortality for pneumonia is up to about 30%, at least if you've got severe pneumonia. That means three out of ten people peg out. Have I got severe pneumonia, or just the old time-honoured run-of-the-mill pneumonia. I've no fucking idea!

I'm rushed to hospital, put on a drip for two days and now I'm shitting myself because I have never been this sick for in all my life.

Panic bells are off the charts now. My brain goes into overdrive. Have I got lung cancer? Are they missing something?

The four-day anxiety levels are off the scale. It's dark, I'm alone, I'm on wires and the beeping is driving me mad because the machine is a warning sign that my lungs are failing

But after many worried nights they say I'm getting better. And now I'm home, but I feel like shit. I'm worried they missed something. My back hurts, and maybe that's a trigger I've got lung cancer. I'm still coughing, not understanding that I have to rest.

So now I'm back to the hospital again and reassured I'm okay. My vitals are good, my back is a little better and I can breathe a sigh of relief.

And this is my life, worrying about my health 24/7. It never lets me rest. I may suddenly have blurred vision that triggers a run to the hospital. I'm a fucking nutcase. But I want to live a long life instead of a doctor saying, "If only you came here a few hours ago we could have saved you"

Welcome to my world.

> So a word of advice from your friendly DJ
> If you want to grow old
> Don't catch a cold

# 78.    Words to Ease Grief

Gladys was a happy soul
Fred was always by her side
They went everywhere together
Their feelings they never hide

Fred worked as builder
Gladys stayed at home
Dinner was always on the table
Her neighbour was lovely Joan

They shared tea and troubles
Laughter and some tears
Joan lived next door to Gladys
Been there forty years

Summer in the garden
Birds had found their song
The phone rang in the hallway
Gladys knew something was wrong

The police had called Gladys
Fred had died in the road
A heart attack they say
They found him on his own

She fell against the kitchen wall
Her legs buckled to the bone
She can't help thinking
That her Fred is not coming home

She screamed the fence to Joan
As time played its part

She fell into her open arms
With her broken heart

Words had no meaning
As Joan dried her tears
It's going to be alright
The words Gladys didn't want to hear

Joan was lost
Not knowing what to say
She just opened up her mouth
And said, Everything's going to be okay

Time is healer
Let's have a cuppa tea
Gladys looked at Joan
And said, I wished you could see

I don't want your words
There's nothing you can say
I know you mean well
But things are not going to be okay

Time is not a healer
In fact, time is full of pain
The fear and dread I feel
That I won't see Fred again

Gladys' world was empty
Just silence and the past
She reflected on time gone by
And how she wished they'd last

She held Joan in her arms
Silence is best said
There is nothing you can say or do
To help bring back my Fred

# 79.    Old Man Stan

I often see the old man
Sitting on his own
A tender looking soul
Seeming all alone

Dressed in a grey suit
Hat and red bowtie
He stares off to the future
Under a beautiful blue sky

Birds sit for company
And feed from his hand
A gentle breeze kisses him
They say his name is Stan

Curiosity got the best of me
I had to say hello
I sat down beside him
There are things I need to know

I started off real slowly
A simple charming chat
He nodded with respect
And took off his hat

We chatted for a while
About the weather and his life
He lost his three children
And finally lost his wife

I find comfort in my solitude
My thoughts dance in my head

Time passed by so quickly
Now all my family are dead

Loneliness finds me
So I walk through the park
I wait until the sun goes down
Be home before it gets dark

He smiled through his sullen eyes
I helped him to his feet
He shuffled down a lonely path
I watched him cross the street

Winter came to London Town
The cold along with the snow
The bench where the old man sat
Where did old Stan go?

I brushed away the frost
And decided to sit a while
An old man sat next to me
And gave me a wonderful smile

It was my old friend Stan
Who drank his homemade tea
I awoke from my dream
That old man was me

# 80.    Puzzled Mind

The man is me with a puzzled mind
So sad the moments of losing time

Broken too is the spirit
The soul hung out to dry
And memories fall like a paper
Planes that can no longer fly

Catch me if fall
Help me catch my breath
I'm slowly losing my sanity
There's not much of me left

# 81.  The Only Sane Moments
## (by Karl)

I witnessed new-born mountain lions in the spring snow

And nomadic elephants crossing the midnight desert.

I remember solitary buzzards flying the grand prairies

And windswept silver pelicans sailing over mudflats.

Slate-grey reef sharks hovering like phantoms above me,

Women chanting from a centuries-old tradition,

And the gypsy girl who let me share her tent.


These were the only sane moments of my life.

## 82.    Let the Music Play

I finally found the secret after all these years of listening to music. I'm sure you'll agree that music has changed from the 40's to today. We've come a long way. Just listen to the styles of today. Of course, we can dance to a beat that moves us, and the beat that helps bounce our body.

But now the secret that will be revealed ......

..... in a moment

The house music that has invaded our feet, and the constant rat-a-tat-tat of the drum beat, and repetitious sounds and added whistles and sampling from James Brown then back to bass line, and yes, you can dance into a trancelike state with the added help of ecstasy or other drugs which intensify the sound. Young kids are drawn to it like moths to a flame. And I'm either old or lost in my own music world, or it's not for me.

Well, my friends, I have found the secret. And it's very simple. It's called emotion and message and love in the lyrics. And tears. That's right, tears, crying over a song. I sat here and tears were streaming down my cheeks just listening to a song. Mainly soul, which is extremely apt with the name - Soul.

'Soul' because it affects you right down to your soul from Marvin Gaye, Billy Paul, Al Green, Otis Redding, The Delfonics, The Ronettes, Barry White, Stylistics, Bobby Womack, The Blackbirds and many more.

There's something about soul music. The writers knew just how to touch you without becoming depressing.

♪♫ Betcha By Golly Wow ♪♫ great song. ♪♫ Sadie ♪♫ by The Spinners. Just simple words and a story that digs into your emotions and make you reflect and simply weep to the writer's hand.

So dig out some Marvin and keep this music alive. The youth of today have drugged their lives away and missed out on the love songs. I don't know what the future holds in music, but what I do know is just like a needle stuck on the vinyl I'm stuck in the 70's soul era.

I do hope it gets more airplay. In the UK there are a few stations that are keeping the old music alive, and the real soul DJs are keeping it real. They know a good thing when they hear it. We may get old, but our soul music is still as fresh as when it was first released

♪♫ Love Town ♪♫ great song. ♪♫ Love Come Down ♪♫ Lovely Day ♪♫ Love Train ♪♫ I'll be Around ♪♫ I'm Doing Fine ♪♫ Girls ♪♫ Rock Creek

Park ♪♫ Movin' ♪♫ Young Hearts Run Free ♪♫ and so many more. I mean many, many more.

As Barry White said, "Let the music play"

# 83.    Take one day at a time

When life is on your shoulders
And broken is your will
Just remember time
Because it won't stand still

Those precious moments wasted
Completely wasted away
You must enjoy the moment
Each and every day

Don't look over your shoulder
Don't look further afield
Stay in the moment
And notice how it feels

Smell flowers in the garden
Relax and take a breath
Don't think about tomorrow
Or wonder how much time is left

Walk into a daydream
Write a poem or read a book
The future will wait for you
There's no reason for you to look

Go see a movie
They say yoga will ease your head
Leave the future to open up
Don't think too far ahead

Stay in the moment
Don't wish your life away

If you worry about tomorrow
It's a price that you must pay

So here is the secret
Dance as much as you can
Sing every day
And never ever plan

Walk where there are fields
Soak up the midday sun
Never give in to age
Always remain young

And yes I am a dreamer
But please listen to what i say
Live your life in the moment
And take it day by day

# 84. Shaking Hands with Tomorrow

We take tomorrow for granted
We plan ahead of time
We laugh away the hours
We never savour the wine

We hurry to arrive nowhere
We run to catch our breath
The race is never over
We're there before we left

Flowers hold their arms out
Roses bloom with age
Oak trees grow with pleasure
Take time to turn your page

Smell and taste the moment
Embrace the sun and moon
Caress a moment's pleasure
For your life may end real soon

Graves hold no malice
Guilt plays a part of life
Crying with mixed emotions
Grief will cut you like a knife

Speak but not of whisper
Cry but not of pain
Laugh when there's no reason
Dance in the pouring rain

Let rainbows through your window
Take time to rest a while

When hurt is on your shoulder
Relax and learn to smile

When you have to say you're sorry
And you're feeling full of sorrow
Don't wait for those excuses
For there may be no tomorrow

## 85.    Be careful what you wish for

No work or money coming in
Jobs have all dried up
Staring out the window
Over my coffee cup

Rent is due by Monday
The bills have got to be paid
Tax season on my shoulder
It's putting me in my grave

Anxiety in the midnight hour
Looking around the room
I need to get to work
I hope my phone rings soon

I'm ready and I'm able
Just need the phone to ring
I can be out the door
And fix anything

It rained for two weeks
As time was passing by
Depression met Anxiety
Thought i was going to die

All my friends were working
Big trucks on the road
My one in the drive way
I had nowhere to go

The wife was moaning everyday
Said, 'Did your phone ring?'
'No love I'm just sitting here

Not a bloody thing'

Then my mate called me
He needed a helping hand
The phone kept on ringing
I was in demand

Then time passed by
And work piled on in
Got to build a balcony
Where do I begin?

Then a demolition job
They need it done right away
Five grand to do it
That's a good week's pay

Now I'm run ragged
My heart can't take anymore
My phone keeps on ringing
As I'm flying out the door

Got to DJ six parties
Do plumbing and build a gate
The owners are getting pissed off
Because I turned up late

Can't even grab a coffee
The home owners can't wait
They want the job finished
How much more can I take

Fell into my arm chair
Then rushed back out the door
There's a moral from this poem
Be careful what you wish for
Phew.

# Dementia

As a handyman, you're privileged to be invited into people's homes and do repairs. But not only that, you're also privileged to be invited into lives for a few minutes. What other people fail to see is the suffering that hides behind the doors of life.

Case in point; my lovely neighbour who needed some work done. I knew he was going through tough times with his wife, who was in the early stages of dementia, but didn't realize the impact it had on him.

So I had to do some repairs and the house was quiet and he told me that he had to put his wife in a care facility due to her dementia. He is heartbroken, and his only salvation is going to the gym for an hour. They were always holding hands and walking the dogs together each morning. But now that's all ended, and all I can see is a broken man who's just holding himself together.

He makes his coffee and stares out the window of a beautiful condo with nothing but loneliness for company. I'm trying to get him to have coffee with me, but he declines and just sits there, lost in thought.

His wife asks for him, and when he visits her she asks who he is. She walks around the care home not knowing where she is, and she fights the nursing staff.

His heart is broken when he leaves her and resumes his own life. So bloody sad to see inside homes that I'm privy to.

I write these few lines to all who are dealing with sadness. Close to home is my lovely sister-in-law, Rita, who struggles every day with ataxia.

So in closing, please take care of each other.

And if you see that item you want, go BLOODY BUY IT. IF YOU WANT A HOLIDAY, GO TAKE IT. PUT IT ON THE CREDIT CARD

Love ya

Take care. I'm off to kiss the kiss while I'm able

# 86.  Love Lies Bleeding

Tom walked down the isle
A shy and hardworking man
A proposal was in the making
When Tom asked for Ruth's hand

Ruth was always a happy girl
A smile that greeted Tom's heart
They went everywhere together
And were very seldom apart

They bought a farm in the country
Tom worked on the land
Forty years together
Just as they had planned

Winter came with sleet and snow
The land was hard to plough
They managed through the bad days
Tom still wonders how

Tom leaned on his shovel
A gaze to melt winter's snow
Far off field of beauty vast
The sunset with its glow

They both sat round the fire
As amber lit the night
They fell asleep in each other's arms
Until the morning night

Tom awoke early
A schedule he had to keep
The animals needed tending
As he let out all the sheep

Days turned to years
Tom knew something was wrong
Ruth was acting very strange
As she forgot the words to a song

She asked Tom what his name was
And the address where they both reside
Tom just smiled with sadness
With the tears he had to hide

Ruth wandered the fields at night
Tom could take no more
He didn't sleep for weeks on end
As Ruth paced up and down the floor

Finally, he sold the farm
A nightmare from a dream
He put Ruth into a nursing home
The pain that no one sees

He put on a painted smile
And tried to hold Ruth's hand
She pulled away with baited breath
And screamed 'Who's this man?'

Tom looked over his shoulder
A final look of grieving
And every step he walked away

To see his love lie bleeding

With special love for all families dealing with Alzheimer's

# 87.     More or Less Touched
# (by Karl)

*"We of the craft are all crazy," observed Lord Byron about himself and his fellow poets. "Some are affected by gaiety, others by melancholy, but all are more or less touched."*

*Danny (the Gypsy Poet, as I call him) has a ferocious spirit and vigour. He has high moods and an instinctive ability to perceive and understand the world around him. Danny has a fierce sense of loyalty, he's romantic, quixotic and starry-eyed. He brings smiles to everyone he meets, a gift I truly believe comes from a higher source. However, at times he can be restless, carrying the capacity for vastly darker moods, melancholy energies and occasional bouts of madness.*

*Most of our Tribe - and in this book you've only met the two of us - but the majority of us are more or less 'touched'. It's what saves us from being mediocre. We sometimes find it disappointing to make friends with people who we simply can't relate to, although we don't necessarily mind this. It's simply that people don't always cut it for us. However, when we're with our tribe it's almost as if the Great Spirit is* saying to us, "Warmer, that's it, you're getting warmer …."

But writers, poets, artists, musicians, prostitutes and circus clowns often suffer from boisterous and raucous dispositions. And it's true they can get us into trouble at times. We wear our moods as our ships of passage, and Danny is no different. He suffers from what Lord Byron would term a "fine madness."

The poems you read in this book, he throws out in a sparkle of energy. Me, it takes me two days or longer to write a poem. Danny can accomplish it in five minutes, and he puts everything into the words. They just arrive on paper as though a higher being is working through him. He has a marvellous sense of the grandiose, but his antithetical moods and energies often form the basis of the artistic disposition and can lead to a manic-depressive frame of mind, all of which, for the artist, can lead to certain advantages such as intense creative potential, enhanced spontaneous reactions and heightened vitality.

I'm not trying to make out that Danny is some kind of mad genius, and I'm certainly not insinuating that it's only writers, artists and musicians who suffer from anxiety and depression. Nor am I trivialising a very real and destructive malady, but you can see how the two go hand-in-hand, can't you?

*Has the reader ever heard of the French poet, Arthur Rimbaud, I wonder. Born in 1854 in Charleville-Mézières, which is a small town located on the banks of the River Meuse, his best works were produced in his late teens and then he gave up creative writing completely when he was about 20. He just dropped out completely. another poet, Paul Verlaine, discovered him living homeless on the streets of Paris. Verlaine was married to 17-year-old Mathilde Mauté de Fleurville, and they had a young son, but he took Rimbaud (pronounced Rim-Beau) home to live with the family, and soon dumped her and jumped into bed with him. Rimbaud, you see, was utterly devoid of the regular moral or sexual restraints that haunt the rest of us. It was a hateful and violent affair, with the two men drinking anise-flavoured absinthe and smoking hashish until the early hours. Eventually Verlaine bought a gun and in a drunken rage shot Rimbaud in the wrist. By the time he was 21, Rimbaud had given up writing altogether. He just lost interest, not even bothering to complete his suite of prose poems, Illuminations, later set to music by Benjamin Britton in an eerie and shadowy chamber suite. Both Bob Dylan and Jim Morrison have expressed appreciation, and punk poet laureate, Patti Smith, has stated that she believes Dylan is the reincarnation of Rimbaud. In fact, Dylan's 'You're Gonna Make Me Lonesome When You Go' makes direct reference to Rimbaud and Verlaine;*

*"Situations have ended sad,*
*Relationships have all been bad.*
*Mine've been like Verlaine's and Rimbaud.*
*But there's no way I can compare*
*All those scenes to this affair,*
*You're gonna make me lonesome when you go"*

*Rimbaud was one of the most influential poets of the 19th century, yet he gave it all up, just walked away. And you'll never guess what happened to him. He became a gun runner in Abyssinia. How mad is that?*

*Yet it's now his story becomes really interesting, for he befriended Emperor Menelik's cousin, Makonnen Wolde Mikael. He was a member of the House of Solomon, the ruling dynasty of the Abyssinian Empire, the members of whom claim direct descent from King Solomon and the Queen of Sheba.*

*I bet the reader didn't know that the joining of humans and Djinni (Genie) in marriage is still practiced in some parts of the world, and the Queen of Sheba was rumoured - by both the Jews and the Arabs - to be part Djinn.*

*Now Haile Selassie, who is revered by Rastafarians as the returned messiah of God, was born Tafari Makonnen Woldemikael, which you'll have to admit isn't a million miles away from Rimbaud's old mate, Makonnen Wolde Mikael.*

In fact, Rimbaud's pal was Haile Selassie's father. Haile Selassie was tutored as a child by a French physician, Dr Vitalien, and a bloke called Abba Samuel, a Capuchin monk of the French Capuchin Mission in Harar, and these two were great mates of Rimbaud. So much so, in fact, that it wouldn't be too much of a stretch of the imagination to appreciate that he had influence not only on the tutors but on their graduate as well.

Trip on that for a minute. Haile Selassie, who Rastafari regard as God, was possibly greatly influenced by a French poet who although he gave up writing at the tender age of 20 (which at first glance appears like a huge waste) must certainly have still held an esoteric, otherworldly mind. It can't have just deserted him, can it? Rimbaud had a bewitching and at times ghoulish psyche which managed to explode out of long-established poetic forms while still in his teens. He did it with more rhythm and beauty than almost anyone you care to name. It's extremely likely that ten years later this man had incredible influence on the child who Rastafari were to later think of as God.

An intriguing thought.

Have you ever heard of François Villon? He was possibly the most prolific French poet of the Middle Ages, and in true Bohemian style he combined poetry and loose living admirably. Born

400 years before Rimbaud he had multiple encounters with the law. Infamous as a member of a wandering bunch of thieves and burglars he was actually banished from Paris on several occasions. His luck finally seemed to have run out in 1461 when he was arrested for brawling and sentenced to the gallows, and it was here that he wrote a piece called Ballad of a Hanged Man. However, a last-minute appeal went through parliament and his sentence was reduced to ten years' banishment from Paris. At the age of 34 he left Paris and was never heard from again. He wrote no more poetry. Just simply vanished as if he really had been beamed up to another planet.

Anthony Bonner, who translated his works into English said, "He might have died on a mat of straw in some cheap tavern, or in a cold, dank cell; or in a fight in some dark street with another French coquillard; or perhaps, as he always feared, on some gallows in a little town in France. We will probably never know." What we do know is that the best-known French poet of the Middle Ages wrote no more poetry as long as he lived, at least not under the name François Villon.

Move forward a few years to 18ᵗʰ century London where we find the inhabitants of the notorious Grub Street, in the Cripplegate ward of London. Believing themselves to be an intellectual proletariat churning out literature of all kinds, but in reality, they were little more than impoverished hack writers and poets, often suffering from starvation, malnutrition, hysteria, delusion and lunacy.

And now think of David Bowie. What a song writer! His brother suffered from schizophrenia, many of his mother's family suffered from a variety of mental illnesses, one of her sisters had also been diagnosed with schizophrenia, a second was in a lunatic asylum because she suffered from clinical depression and, no doubt, schizophrenia too, and she had another sister who'd undergone a lobotomy to cure her mental issues. Nowadays everybody dances around the euphemisms terming them emotional collapse, neurasthenia, clinical depression, melancholia, major affective disorder, manic-depressive psychosis, bipolar or just a simple basket case. However, back then, you were 'mentally handicapped' and that was it. Bowie thought they were all nuts and always had a haunting fear that the 'family nuttiness' as he termed it was in his genes also. It probably was.

How weird is that? Out of the chaos of their lives, these poets force other's hearts to roar in a way that is magnificent!

"Follow your inner moonlight," said Beat Poet Allen Ginsberg, "Don't hide the madness."

"Most poets are young simply because they have not been caught up. Show me an old poet and I'll show you, more often than not, either a madman or a master" Charles Bukowski

"Imperfection is beauty, madness is genius and it's better to be absolutely ridiculous than absolutely boring" Marilyn Monroe

So, is there a relationship between ingenuity, inspiration and emotional disorders? Possibly. I think it's true that certain lifestyles give elbow-room to extremes in behaviour and mood. And the variety of moods, their fluctuations if you like, can easily inflame thought-changing concepts, leading to romantic and expressive language.

But I repeat what I said a few pages ago, I'm not insinuating that it's only poets, misfits, writers, mystics, heretics, painters or troubadours who suffer from tension, worry or despair. Nor am I trivialising a very genuine and devastating illness, but you can see how the two go hand-in-hand, can't you?

## 88.   Robin Williams

Madness wakes me each morning
It whispers in my head
The world kisses me awake
It helps me get out of bed

My stage of loneliness
The laughter that fills the abyss
And twisted are the demons
That constantly persist

The voices without reason
They tempt my broken will
And sadness plays her part so well
No one knows how I feel

A mask that covers my intentions
A walk that's mine to take
And silence echoes in my head
I know many hearts will break

My coat of many colours
A smile that hides my pain
Thoughts of suicide take control
I'm the one to blame

A handle from an open door
A knot I tied so well
Around my neck I tied the rope
And this is where I fell

I take my final curtain call
My feelings I had to hide
To all I send this message
DONT HIDE SUICIDE

## 89.  Having a rough day? (by Karl)

*Place your hand on your heart. Feel that? That's called intention! You're alive for a reason. Don't quit now.*

*Remember; you've survived 100% of your worst days so far.*

*And whatever happens you'll never have to do today again. You cracked today, and that's a solid effort. It may not have been easy, I know. And tomorrow might not be easy either. But at least it won't be today.*

*Feel that 'intention' in your heart. And just in case no one's ever told you, you're beautiful, you're loved and you're needed. You're more capable, and more powerful, and actually more energetic than you think. You're going to get through this*

*In the words of that great philosopher, Winnie the Pooh, "You're braver than you believe, stronger than you seem and smarter than you think."*

# 90. Depression (by Karl)

*And always remember that depression is smaller than you. You were here first. It exists within you, not the other way around. Remember that.*

# 91.    Anxiety

I just want to talk briefly again about Anxiety, because that's what this book's about. I hope my poems entertain you, but I'll continue to voice me feelings. If the topic of Anxiety doesn't concern you then …. Well … I don't know how you stumbled on this book in the first place. But if you ever feel panicky, weird, strange and have trouble dealing with life I want to stress again and again that you're not alone. It's frightening, but quite normal

I have been to hell and had to hide it

I remember when my dog died, I had to DJ that night in front of 200 people. I thought it couldn't get any worse, then Mum and Dad died, then more family members died, then my best friend Chalkie was murdered, and it was then that ANXIETY AND DEPRESSION came alive and nearly killed me

The fear waits in the morning. Just fear. It's a real condition. But with the help of friends who don't laugh at me or say 'snap out of it' I'm getting there

The doors of Anxiety have been closed for many years, and silent sufferers have been left in the dark, trying to figure out what the hell is going on.

Your heart is the signal that sends you to hospital because it's beating fast, or should I say POUNDING for no reason. Your body has a fight & flight button that just gets switched on and then ALL HELL BREAKS LOOSE. It can be triggered by a friend dying (or in my case a friend being murdered), or perhaps health issues no matter how small. And it can be very frightening. If you're alone, you feel like you're going to die

I'm sharing these feelings to help you (and myself, I guess) deal with this bloody disorder. I hold no shame or embarrassment. My friend, and co-author, Karl, is helping to collaborate my thoughts for this book, because they're all jumbled and fucked up in my head, as if a serpent is winding through the labyrinth of my mind, throwing mad thoughts and beliefs at me as I stand unrobed, defenceless and vulnerable. I dance around my bones on the edge of existence and all I feel is a fierce urgency.

I have, it's true, a cluttered mind.

After the decomposition of flesh all I have is the boneyard colour of my mind. I know I suffer from excessive ideation, as if a swarm of wasps are flying round and round in my mind, but I don't know what the fuck to do about it. Wasps and serpents and madness and a plethora of thoughts. My mind is a rolling stone and I feel like when Chalkie died all he left us was alone (to borrow a line from The Temptations).

I'm no expert, just a sufferer. I have no idea how this condition came on. I was laughing through life, then family and friends died. I think my best friend getting killed was the tipping point. My brain could not conceive death due to a murder, but the switch was turned on and all hell broke loose. I don't expect you to understand, but if psychic tension has never tapped on your door, trust me, don't open it. You cannot control it. It controls you, and all you're left with is that hollow feeling of being lost and alone. There are many tablets you can take, and walks and hiking and yoga classes, but once it gets hold of you it's a bastard, a controlling bastard

So the secret is written

I write many poems and shit like that and, trust me, it helps me. Music helps a lot. And I also tell people that the mask we all hide behind will only help for so long. It's time for you to come out from behind it and talk to someone. When people meet me they have no idea that I'm hiding behind a mask.

But I'm getting better. I'm getting a handle on it. I'm still holding on

To understand Anxiety is not a job for the faint-hearted

## 92.   Keep Busy

Keep clear of coffee and alcohol. A glass after dinner is only natural, and accepted socially, but too much coffee or alcohol or drugs is going to fuck you up. It leaves you defenceless. Instead watch a movie, keep positive, open windows and doors and let fresh air in. Play music.

But most of all, keep busy. I try and keep busy because I'm afraid if I don't I'll sink. Force yourself to exercise. You feel much better after a good workout. Help a friend or a neighbour. And even if you're doing the same thing daily, try to incorporate a new twist into it. Drive a different route or something, but most of all keep busy and talk to friends.

# 93.    Anxiety (by Karl)

*Anxiety is a smoking, snorting, sniffing species of
mental trauma
It is the colour of fireworks and drive-by-
shootings
Of fratricide and dust
Anxiety is an illness of decomposition.*

*It is upheaval
Causing sudden and violent change
The irrevocable end towards which all life moves
The determination of mankind's ultimate fate at
the end of the world.*

*Anxiety presides over the moment of a man's
birth
Spinning out the events and actions of his life
And cutting its thread with shears.*

*Anxiety is a church key, large and flat with a
triangular head
The three sides representing the three sisters of
fate.*

*Anxiety is the handwriting on the wall
It is scrawl and scribble and chicken tracks
It is an illness that dogs its heels in and leaves
no stone unturned.*

*It is a pack of wolves degraded by non-
productivity and shiftlessness
It is the colour of tramps and beggars and
criminals.*

*Anxiety is a smoking gun.*

# 94.     Jet (by Karl)

*Jet is the colour of alley juice*
*And mad dog wine.*

*It is a screwloose, schizzed out, psycho of a colour*
*A colour for cutting out paper dolls.*

*It is the colour of intense mental pain*
*Of tortured states of mind.*

*Jet is the colour of distress*
*Of unease*
*Of apprehension*
*Of psychic tension.*

*Jet is a state of confusion*
*Of disordered speech*
*Of hallucination and frenzy.*

*It is a colour for popping the clutch*
*And driving off in a brand-new Cadillac.*

*Jet is the colour of hamburgers sizzling on an open grill.*

## 95.     Leather (by Karl)

*Leather is a dark and dusky colour.*
*A raven-haired, black-eyed colour that could eat*
*the arsehole out of a bear.*

*It is also the back-alley colour of funk-fusion*
*And low-down dirty jam sessions*
*The colour of slurred gut-bucket riffs*
*Smooth and mellow.*

*It is the colour of soul and ragtime and gospel.*

*Leather-coloured music is also jug band and*
*Cajun blues and scat.*

*Leather is a swamp rat with a gris-gris bag.*

# 96.    White Coat Dealer or Doctor

I take more pills than an addict
I wash them down with pain
My symptoms get worse
So back to my dealer again

He comes out in a white coat
An impression that I like
How's it going, Mr Winter?
Is everything alright?

Well doc, I got this pain
And it just won't go away
He writes me out a prescription
It says take four tablets every day

Then the trouble started
The side effects were worse
Then my wife became my doctor
Digging pills out from her purse

My head started spinning
The couch became my bed
My anxiety was kicking in
I thought that I was dead

Sweating like a stuffed pig
I was feeling really ill
Then in comes the neighbour
And says take one of my pills

Now I'm flying like concord
And I don't know where I am

I put one foot on the floor
And try to bloody stand

That's when the floor hit me
And I was on my back
I knew something was wrong
So I went back to see my quack

Nice to see you again, Mr Winter
What seems to be so wrong
Those tablets that you gave me
They seem to be very strong

Your body has to get used to them
In fact, you should take more
You need to take six a day
Instead of taking four

So now I'm seeing dinosaurs
They're climbing up the walls
I'm scratching like a monkey
And I can't even feel my balls

So now I called my doctor
You have an infection in your sack
I'm going to give you other tablets
So there's no need for you to come back

I take tablets for blood pressure
And some I take for pain
I take tablets to thin my blood
So it don't block up my veins

I take tablets for anxiety
And one for my heart
I take six tablets in the morning
Before my day can start

I don't like getting older
It's hard as hell to survive
Thank God I got my doctor
Who is keeping me alive

So when you see your doctor
And you feel your life is at an end
Just remember this poem
Make sure your doctor is your friend

# 97. Part Two of White Coat Dealer (by Karl)

But then again, I wonder
What's the truth behind these pills
Maybe that doctor made a blunder
The medicine's giving me the chills

For that's how he earns his money
That double-dealing quack
I bet he thinks it's funny
He doesn't intend that I bounce back

I've seen him so many times
And all he does is assure me
I'm now suspecting his crimes
He never intends to cure me

For supposing I was cured
I'd tell him to stuff his pills
I wouldn't need to be assured
And he couldn't live in Beverley Hills

## 98.　　Gerbil on the Wheel

Late one winter's night
I wasn't feeling very well
I couldn't catch my breath
And my face had started to swell

No problem for this hero
It will simply go away
But the symptoms got worse
Day after day

Started telling people
That something was wrong
They just laughed over the noise
And said put another tune on

Then in walked Jim Dupree
A lovely Scottish man
Said for fuck's sake Danny
Go to hospital fast as you can

So I braved the white coats and nurses
They put me on a machine
We need to keep you overnight
We don't like what's seen on the screen

Early Monday morning
They prepared me for the news
You have a blockage in your heart
And there's no time to lose

Then the surgeon advised me
Listen to your heart

If it ever stops beating
It's going to be hard to start

So after my procedure
The gerbil was on the wheel
Every day worrying
And wondering if I'm really ill

If I get indigestion
I'm in hospital with the pain
Then anxiety kicks in
And it starts all over again

I'm on this bloody treadwheel
Worrying about my cough
Back to the doctors once again
I think he's had enough

So when does one go to the doctor
Should you simply wait
Or leave it to a higher power
And resign yourself to fate

Not a chance in heaven
Not a chance in hell
I'm going straight to see my doctor
If I start to feel unwell

You only have a golden hour
If you suffer a heart attack
Go and see your doctor
Before you're lying on your back

# 99.    Health & Wealth

I can't run like I used to
Those days have passed me by
I'm not as strong as I used to be
And my emotions make me cry

My children have grown and gone
Just shadows on a wall
And books that pile on a shelf
The ones my kids took to school

The silence of my noisy brain
The darkness of the night
And time dances like butterflies
As all my memories take flight

Pictures of a long-lost youth
Remind me not to get old
And chasing rainbows in my sleep
Looking for that pot of gold

My smile will forever haunt me
My hands held my fate
And wasted moments I threw away
How I thought time could wait

But alas I've found solace
A peace that calms the soul
I take a slice of happiness
And try not to let it go

I walk where there is sunshine
I even laugh in the rain
I kiss the sky from time to time

It takes away the pain

I hold hands with my shadow
I dance when there is no song
And friends remind me how lucky I am
It helps me to remain strong

Take care of each other
Most of all take care of yourself
But remember just how rich you are
While you still have your health

# 100.  Along came the Cell Phone

We used to go to dinner
And chat all through the night
She smiled through my innocence
And held me real tight

We made love for hours
And stayed in bed a day long
Next thing I know
She brings the cell phone along

We don't talk anymore
She's always on the phone
We sit in the restaurant
I might as well be alone

Then she starts texting
The dinner's getting cold
She smiles across her wine glass
And I'm getting old

She then has to go outside
Susan wants to chat
She comes back later
Says Sue split up with Matt

Finally she puts the phone down
Waiter my food is cold
She won't listen to a word I said
This girl won't be told

Then the phone rings again
She's speaking whilst she eats
I'm just sitting there
Watching food chew in her cheeks

'Really, no really
What are you going to do?
I'll call you back later
I'm just finishing off my food'

Finally I get to speak to her
She smiles once again
She goes to the rest room
So I take out my pen

I wrote on the napkin
I have to go home
The only way I'll talk to you
Is when you're on the phone

So this is my message
Treat your date like a star
When you're in a restaurant
Leave your cell phones in the car

# 101.  My Wife is a Party Girl

She waits with a ragging smile
Beneath a venom of hate
She screams from the kitchen
You didn't wash up your plate

She flies off the handle
Like a witch on a broom
And a voice to wake the dead
Clean up the bloody room

Bloodcurdling cries
From a mouth that looks so sweet
When you're in the toilet
Will you put down the bloody seat

Then an almighty bang
She slams the cupboard door
How many times must I tell you
Don't leave your clothes on the floor

Then I hear her leaving
I tip-toe across the room
I see that she has gone
But I know she'll be back soon

So I make a cup of coffee
And I cut a nice slice of cake
She comes back a little early
That was my biggest mistake

She roars like a lion
There's crumbs on the sink
I spin for excuses

And had no time to think

I said I'm about to clean up
Just as you came in
She launched into a rocket
And threw cake wrappers in the bin

Trying to watch the telly
Her sarcastic points of view
Ain't you working today Danny
Ain't there something you can do ?

She pours herself a glass of wine
The red I hate to see
Because it's just like blood
And she's coming after me

Then the wine kicks in
As she open up her claws
A little sarcastic comment
And I'm looking for the doors

I'm out of here in any second
She's about to explode
Her eyes turn to red
Now It's time for me to go

She rattles like a snake
A shot across the bow
She gives me a little warning
As her hair falls on her brow

I can still hear her voice
From a sweet Irish girl
You promised me diamonds
And take me round the world

By now she's staggering
As Carolyn gets the call
She can hear everything
Coming through the wall

Then Sonia hears the battle cry
They both roll up their sleeves
I'm like Custer at the Bighorn
It was now time for me to leave

Carolyn was ready
An empty glass in hand
Sonia was the backup
Just as they had planned

Then in walks Ellie
And Dusty by her side
Corks were popping one by one
It was like fourth of bloody July

Then the gossip got on its way
Of course, I'm to blame
I'm just looking through the window
Watching the smoke turn to flame

Then the party started
As the wine started to flow
Then more girls came in
They're the last ones to know

Then the call went out
And more girls started to arrive
They all joined in the song
Of course, ♫ I will survive ♫

Colette's singing to Abba
The girls are singing along

They're all pissed out their heads
Forgetting the words to the song

I came back seven hours later
The calmness of the night
The exorcist came to mind
As Colette still wanted to fight

Her head spun off her shoulders
Her lips were red with wine
I tried to sneak on by her
Another mistake of mine

Where the hell have you been?
As she drank her vino dry
That was when their time was up
And all the girls said goodbye

And there laid my sweetheart
Passed out on the bed
She sleeps with both eyes open
I thought that she was dead

Then I heard her moaning
I knew she was going to be okay
The best thing to keep her happy
Is just keep out her way

# 102.    Note from Karl

*I have to stress that Danny wrote the poem above by simple insight, the kind that is never offered by generalisation. Danny's beautiful wife, Colette, is very supportive, but in 'My Wife is a Party Girl' he's nailed it. Who knows why women look to find so many faults in their men?*

*"You've got grease all over the pan" (an opportunity to blame the man for something and to cause ill feelings where there's no need)*

*"That's right, we did get grease (the man shoulders half the blame) from when we (she) cooked sausages and bacon yesterday. I was going to clean it all up after breakfast" (he's trying to be a good bloke here, and not create bad blood or acrimony)*

*"It's not from the sausages and bacon yesterday. I put greaseproof paper down and cleared that up. I've only used it for hot-cross buns. There will have only been a few crumbs"*

*"Okay (the man's getting blamed once again for something he didn't do), well it's not from my toast, but I'll clean it up after breakfast, don't worry" (trying to bring the unnecessary situation that SHE has caused to a close)*

A tut and a sigh from the woman, which he hates; "Whatever, I'm not arguing about grease in a pan, Christ!"

But she IS arguing about grease in a pan, isn't she? There was no need for her to say anything at all, but she did so because it was an opportunity to cause ill feelings in the marriage. Women do this all the time, bring something up just to cause an argument when it would be much more conciliatory not to say anything at all. She could have said nothing at all, she knows he'll clear it up, he always does, but it was too good an opportunity to miss, even though it was her that cooked the sausages and bacon. But now that she's started the argument she's really pissed off AT HIM because SHE left grease all over the pan, and by being a nice guy about it she's even more pissed off at him. I don't know why women get pissed off at guys for being nice to them and for trying not to cause agitation, but they do.

So to turn the situation around that SHE started, she now blames HIM for causing an argument about something SHE'S guilty of herself. But the truth is, he didn't. He was just getting his breakfast. He'd noticed the grease in the pan, but he wasn't going to say anything about it. He just intended to clean it up after breakfast, which was okay, but she doesn't want it to be okay, it's too good an opportunity to let go.

So what does she do? She blames him for causing the argument when five minutes earlier he was just getting on with his breakfast unaware that an argument was heading his direction.

Women do this all the time to men. The guy will be quite relaxed and happy, not focusing on anything in particular, maybe watching a bit of television, when she'll suddenly ask him a question from the other room that he has no idea how to answer; "Do you think I should put this thing behind the plant pot?"

What thing?

Which plant pot?

Why?

Why not put it somewhere else?

What is she talking about?

She knows all this, of course, but is enjoying his confusion. And the man is now thinking, "What can I answer that won't piss her off?"

This happens all the time to men. And the truth is there's no answer that won't piss her off because of the way she's phrased it. For some unknown reason women, with their belligerent and cantankerous natures, thrive on causing ill feelings. A number of men face quite a deal of conflict or even confrontation of one type or another at work, and the last thing they want is conflict at home. But she's not going to let him get away with that, and he's now thinking, "If I say this, she'll probably get pissed off, but if I answer that, then that's also going to annoy her. How did this happen? Why does she do this? What fucking thing? Which plant pot?"

"Which thing?" There you go, he's asked a question to try and narrow it down a little bit.

A tut and a sigh and a roll of the eyes from her because he's so inept. "We talked about it yesterday," and she explains it to him as if he's an idiot.

I've no idea why women do this to men. It seems that they just like the confrontation, but there really is no need for it. The guy wants to relax after a hard day's work, but if there's an opportunity to cause acrimony or resentment then she'll jump at it. She'll even go looking for it.

It may possibly be because women back away from confrontation at work. They're nice to everyone at work, even the ones who piss them off, so they want to take it out on someone, and who better than the poor sucker she married. Whereas men are completely opposite. They deal with their conflicts at work and don't bring them home with them.

*The guy just wants an easy life at home, he wants it to be a pleasant place, but whatever he does seems to piss her off.*

*"Are you cooking bacon?"*

*There's no answer to this because he's cooking bacon. And he now knows from experience that if he admits to having bacon in the pan she'll use that to have a pop at him about something. But bacon's sizzling away and he can hardly deny it, can he?*

*"Yeah, do you want some?"*

*He's being nice about it. He feels sure that something about him cooking bacon will have pissed her off, or maybe she just wants to use it as an excuse for an argument, but he's trying to diminish the situation.*

*"Well, you've opened a new packet of bacon. We always keep the bacon in the Tupperware container." And there we have it. She knew he was cooking bacon, the aroma of frying bacon is impossible to miss, but it was a good excuse to have a pop at him. He's only been up five minutes and already he's in trouble.*

*So we have a situation here whereby the man does everything he can not to annoy her, he just wants an easy home life, but she seems to do everything SHE can to annoy HIM, because she thrives on battle at home. I don't know why.*

*What I do know, though, is that it can lead to depression in the man*

*Just like Danny's poem above, she seems to enjoy a few glasses of wine or gin with the girls more than time spent with the man. Not only that, but she seems to trust them more. She'll talk to them about all sorts, yet when he asks about what some may term 'personal matters' she says, "Oh, I find that difficult to talk about," even though he's the one person she should be talking to about it*

*So the poor bloke ends up going from situation to situation whereby not only is he kept out of the loop but he now finds himself thinking, "What can I say that won't annoy her?" and the fact that he's pondering over it for a second or two still annoys her. He can't win.*

*So Danny's poem above is on the money. Spot on*

## 103.  One Day We'll all be Photographs

Found a box of photographs
Faces without a care
Many years later
Some of those faces are not there

Gone with Father Time
Memories are all that's left
Those faces stare back at me
Now heartache and regrets

The nights were full of laughter
The mirror danced as well
And lipstick red was all the rage
Memories I wouldn't sell

Empty promises made at night
Holding your shoes in your hand
Dancing the night away
To your favourite band

Alas time to say goodbye
Lay your photographs to rest
Keep out one old photograph
And lay it on your chest

We all see empty faces
When we venture to the past
Nothing is forever
Even time doesn't last

Just remember this story Rita

And remember you're not alone
We all will be in photographs
For one day we'll all be gone

A Man from the Stars

They say he walks on water
Turns water into wine
Man of very few words
They say he's so de vine

He's humble with passion
A heart that has no hate
Gentle as flower
Knows destiny and fate

He see a world of wonder
Magical, amazed and awe
His garden that he walks in
Has many open doors

He see light where there is shade
He heals the meek and lame
A mystery of a man
No one knows his name

He leaves you with his shadow
A window to his soul
He spreads the joy of love
And peace is his goal

He walks with a whisper
He never shouts at all
He listens with his heart
He will answer when you call

I call him Star Gazer

A mystic of the night
Hold his hand to the Promised Land
He will walk you to the light

# 104.   An Old Man and His Book

Summer came to California
The sea kissed the shore
I laid back on a summer's day
Who could ask for anything more?

I sipped the summer juices
And life was on the breeze
Young girls in small bikinis
Laying under palm trees

The sweet scent and their beauty
Their youth was plain to see
They held time in both their hands
Alas no time for me

Seagulls danced with paper
They never show their age
I stare across a field of sand
As I slowly turn the page

Trembling are my weary hands
A life that fell from grace
I ran through life so very fast
I thought it was all a race

And seldom do I stand anymore
My legs are far behind
And feeble as I so might be
How life can be so unkind

I read to keep the cobwebs at bay
The cogs that twist and grind
Thank God for my eyesight
Without it I'd lose my mind

No matter the age that befalls me
And all the chances that I took
You know where you can find me
On the beach with bloody good book

# 105.   The Bench

Maggie sits everyday
On a bench that's weary and old
She brings along her blanket
It stops her feeling the cold

Church bells ring on a Sunday morn
She brings flowers to a grave
A man she loved for sixty years
And by his side she's stayed

Tammy lies at her feet
A love she won't let die
She brushes away wind swept leaves
And also wipes her eyes

Good morning Tammy, my love
She whispers to a stone
Sorry I was late today
I hate for you to be alone

Maggie welcomes the silence
The solitude of the day
And broken as her heart may be
It's a price that she must pay

Two sparrows keep her company
Few crumbs she brings alone
They greet her every morning
And thank her with a song

A lady sat beside her
Her husband too had passed

She stared off to better days
The ones she thought would last

The bench held many memories
The wood stained with tears
It's lasted two world wars
Been here for many years

Maggie shared her story
Time took Tammy away
Cancer shared their hopes and dreams
He died on Christmas Day

Time had come to say goodbye
They're going to lock the gate
Maggie looked over her shoulder
Telling Tammy she won't be late

She shuffled off to loneliness
A heart without a fence
Tomorrow will find her once again
Sitting on the bench

## 106.   Don't Forget to Live

Brought flowers to a graveside
They too will also die
Caught tears on my white shirt
The ones I tried to hide

No words or sermon
Will reunite your loss
Death is beside all of us
And tomorrow's what we've lost

The future seems far away
As today passes by
The clock keeps its time well
As the seconds start to fly

So run and cram your life in
Don't walk and take it slow
They say take it easy
You still have a long way to go

I disagree whole heartedly
Run as fast as you can
Smell as many flowers
For life hasn't got a plan

Taste all the sampled fruits
Dance the night and day
Take a moment's silence
For friends that passed away

Then open up as many doors
Laugh when there are tears

Face your demons one by one
Never show your fears

Let night time hold its secrets
For shadows won't leave a mark
Light will guide you through bad times
And take you out of the dark

Go catch that rainbow
Find silver and crusted gold
Live your life as fast as you can
Before you get bloody old

# 107.   A Soldier's Story

Michael was the first born
A gentle loving lad
He fought his way through childhood
But he'd give everything he had

He joined the army at seventeen
To make his family proud
He passed with flying colours
And he stood out from the crowd

He was soon made leader
They sent him off to war
They sent him to a country
He had never been before

Dead babies in the rubble
Women torn to shreds
Men blown to pieces
Many with no heads

The mayhem and the killings
The sound of screams and cries
Children lost in gunfire
As they watch their parents die

Time stood still for a while
As his men caught their breath
A mine exploded by their truck
There was only Michael left

Medics came and saved him
Flew him back to base
It was only when he got home

Michael saw he'd lost his face

One arm was missing
Part of his leg as well
Shrapnel pierced his lung
And his life is a living hell

One year in hospital
The scars too are deep inside
He moved out on the streets
And no one heard him cry

Forgotten by his government
His smile would break your heart
He remembers all his comrades
That were all blown apart

The dark screams of nightmares
The phone that never rings
He sits alone in his head
Listening for angels to sing

Alas a man with a broken will
Sad and all alone
A soldier waits for death to come
And finally take him home

Then early one morning
A broken box for a home
A soldier in a wheelchair
Said "I heard you're all alone"

They shared their war stories
The sadness and the pain
Tommy was the soldier
And said he'd be back again

Two weeks to the very day
Tommy sat outside
He bought with him two hundred soldiers
And they all stood by his side

We have come to help you Michael
No need to be afraid
You laid your life for queen and country
For this you should be paid

Now Michael lives with many friends
And never shall be alone
Michael finds old soldiers
And gets them into homes

This is a true story
For our soldiers die on our streets
Many can't find a home
Or get very much to eat

And while we share our holidays
And wrap up in our beds
Give a thought to our soldiers
Especially the ones that are dead

My heart breaks for all of you
With love and Jesus Christ
Thank you for your service
And your ultimate Sacrifice

# 108.   The Gift of Life

The world is wonderful
For the lucky and the few
She sips on her latte
Wondering what she'll do

She might go shopping with Susan
Have her nails done in the mall
Might buy some new shoes
Need to give her mother a call

My God this weather is awful
It's always hot and dry
She said she needs a holiday
But she hates to bloody fly

The gardener is late again
The grass needs a trim
This is the second time
She's going to have a word with him

Having cocktails in Malibu
Laying by the pool
It's getting quite boring
What's a girl to do?

Far away in Africa
In a village time forgot
A young girl dances every day
On her head she carries a pot

The rain adds to her beauty
Her smile the world can't see
She has hardly any possessions
Because everything is free

The stars come out to greet her
The sun kisses her face
Mother Earth whispers
Life is not a race

Her village has no hunger
They kill only what they eat
There's no need for fashion
Just sandals on her feet

I ask her of her secret
What is the best gift you can give
She looked into my deep blue eyes
Said show people how to live

My arms are always open
I give thanks for what I have
Life is the most precious gift
And riches will make you sad

She showed me a diamond
Been in the village for many years
So many wars fought over this
Left our people in tears

She held out both her hands
One held out food
The other was the diamond
She said which one do you choose?

We have no need of diamonds
We have no need of gold
You cannot eat these items
For treasure is growing old

Food will fill your body
Water will quench your thirst

Life is for living
And greed is but a curse

Give love where there is hatred
Show passion where there is pain
Teach the gift of friendship
And try not to complain

Listen with an open heart
Embrace where there was doubt
Find compassion in everyone
Don't leave anyone out

I said goodbye with a tear in my eye
For now I am rich at heart
This lady taught me well
Can't wait for my life to start

# 109.  Madness into Hell

She cries over her coffee cup
A woman that time forgot
She brushed her hair with her fingers
But didn't know when to stop

She stood in her empty room
A bed with leather straps
She banged her head against the wall
Until she finally collapsed

Her screams made your skin crawl
Her demons danced in her head
And night time had a feast
As her madness had to be fed

Walls white as clean sheets
A peep hole in the door
A corridor led the way
As she paced across the floor

Morning Miss Becky
A reaction with faraway eyes
She crawled into her corner
To the sound of her own cries

Visitors were far and few
Just her mother of sixty one
Becky was an only child
When her mother lost her son

Becky took her brother fishing
On a beautiful summer's day
The sun kissed the water

Just down by Studland Bay

Michael was only nine-years-old
As they fished along the bank
Michael fell into the sea
As Becky's heart also sank

She never had the courage
To save her brother's life
She carries that reminder
Each and every night

And so her mind became twisted
As madness took control
She never saved her brother's life
And time has taken its toll

Becky died all alone
Her mother died as well
The sadness of a broken mind
And madness into hell

## 110.    Forgotten Family

Time to take stock
Realise what I had
I left home so young
I also left mum and dad

The road greeted me
With youth at my feet
The sun on my shoulder
Life was so sweet

The rain didn't bother me
The world in my hands
Tomorrow was my future

I didn't need any plans

But time took its toll
And age played her part
The loss of my parents
Broke this young boy's heart

I looked over my shoulder
What have I done?
I forgot my family
When I left home so young

Now I'm older
I'm weary and sad
I didn't realize
What I really had

Aunties and uncles
Have not been seen for so long
Cousins and nephews
Many are gone

I reflect on my life
And what would I give
To turn back the clock
But it's all RELATIVE


The truth of it all, however, is that if I hadn't left home I'd more than likely be in prison by now. We were all going down the wrong path.

Love ya

Danny

## 111.  Met Gladys at the Bus Stop

Rained cats and dogs
Waiting for the bus
Lovely old lady sat next to me
Just the two of us

She looked down at the ground
A gentle loving soul
I whispered in a soft voice
Where do you have to go?

I go to the cemetery
To visit my husband jack
He died in the war
But only his body came back

I go every weekend
And sit down by his stone
He went to war at nineteen
And only his soul came home

He was my only love
I wear black everyday
I can still remember the day
That Jack went away

We were going to have a holiday
When he came home from the war
But time took its toll
And there was a knock upon my door

Sorry to inform you
A letter from the crown
Jack went missing in combat

When his plane was shot down

She held onto her hanky
And wrapped it around her hand
Life is so uncertain
And not how we had planned

I'm ninety-seven in just a few days
My memories take me back
The only wish I have to make
Is to be buried next to my jack

Out from the distance
The bus suddenly arrived
I helped her on her way
And waved to her goodbye

She left behind a photo
Of a handsome looking man
Dressed in an Air Force uniform
And standing by a pram

On the back was written
Jack and Baby Jack
But written on the envelope
Sorry but your letter was sent back

Many nights I never slept
A photo of sad regret
I want to give it back to Gladys
The lady that I just met

I waited by the bus stop
In the pouring rain
Hoping to find her
And see her once again

Up in the distance
A saddened-looking face
She was looking for her photo
Searching all over the place

Her eyes lit with wonder
As I gave her photo back
Now she was back together
With her husband Jack

# 112. Birthdays

If you are normal, then you are mad. It's impossible to live your life without worrying

What I mean by that is that youth plays its part and age is just a birthday. Age is cake, candles, hats and laughter. Then as time throws you forward you're a little wiser and still able to climb stairs. The problem is we become a sponge and suck up ailments and worry, then we convince ourselves it's serious.

That's just the start. Then throw in the bills, then another bloody birthday comes along with lines and wrinkles, then the sponge keeps soaking up more and more. The birthdays are quicker, then friends die, and your own mortality comes into question

Don't any of you dare tell me that you're not affected by age, health, money etc. because if you're not then your bloody MAD

Love ya

# 113.   I will never leave you

This is a quick poem about a woman who never left her man's side after a horrific accident. Very sad. He is still recovering, with her help and vigil.

We took our vows as lovers do
For better or for worse
And time changed overnight
And life became a curse

That fateful night of tragedy
A moment of despair
To your side I ran to you
A promise to always be there

Doctors faces said it all
As I ran to your side
Machines held your breath
And I died inside

Life became so cruel
The waiting and the pain
Will you ever see me?
Will you ever speak my name?

The nights were nightmares
God had made me wait
And tears found their home
And rage turned to hate

But time had kept her promise

A vigil I had to keep
I watch over you at night
And watch you while you sleep

And through it all you made it
A sparkle back to life
Words were whispered slowly
And I was still your wife

The road ahead awaits us both
But somehow you made it through
We're making plans to marry again
So I can say 'I do'

# 114.   White Powder Junkie

I'm a white powder junkie, meaning I'm a sugar addict. I love sugar. I put it in and on everything. Can't do without it. They said try Sweet 'n' Low. Turns out saccharine can give you cancer. Sugar can give you diabetes. What's a man with a sweet tooth to do?

I've got the answer. Goodbye sugar, hello Liquid Stevia Organic. Two drops and I'm in Heaven, sweet as a nut, no calories and safe

So anyway, just in case you're interested, go check it out.

Thanks to my lovely daughter, I'm sugar free.

## 115.   She Kissed me with her Eyes

I played around from town to town
A moment I shall never forget
It was in the summer of '78
The summer of regret

Music filled the hearts and souls
Also filled the floors
As perfumed ladies danced away
And boys leaned against the walls

She smiled across the room
A look to melt ice or snow
A kiss she blew to me
As I watched her go

A madness I can't explain
A meeting in the stars
She looked back over her shoulder
And stepped into her car

She kissed me with her eyes
The time I shall never forget
If only I had run to her
Now my life is of regret

Scattered memories wait for me
I can still see her face
A smile into tomorrow
She's gone without a trace

Darkness into a blinded storm

A reflection that plays her part
Here stands a man dying
With a broken heart

Morning rushes to my side
A window that hides my pain
Her eyes I can still see clearly
How I would love to see them again

Dreams do come true
But some I should forget
I have finally found those eyes
In my beautiful Colette

## 116.   Nursing Home Alone

Just went into a nursing home to price a job.
Here's my poem:


The halls of white paint
The nurses white as well
Lunch time in the cafeteria
I hated the bloody smell

A man was in his nineties
His world was passing by
Saw two little old ladies
One was about to die

Age is cruel and heartless
My rage at father time
The bastard of getting older
All of us stand in line

They all wait for the Grim Reaper
Each day comes at a cost
They wake up each morning
Cursing another loss

The TV keeps them company
If only for a while
Soaked in their own piss
They still manage a smile

How I fear what awaits me
The waiting room of death

The sadness in those sullen eyes
And wonder who just left

Don't tell me about my anxiety
This will break your heart
Old and left all alone
Many in the dark

I saw an old lady
Trying to catch her breath
I called a nurse to help her
But they said everyone had left

I wish we were born a hundred
Then get younger every day
Instead of dying old
We would be young as we pass away

I know this poem is depressing
But if you saw what I saw
I know that most of you
Would have never walked through that door

# 117.   I walked a mile with Pleasure (by Robert Browning Hamilton)

*I walked a mile with Pleasure*
*She chatted all the way*
*But left me none the wiser*
*For all she had to say.*

*I walked a mile with Sorrow,*
*And ne'er a word said she*
*But, oh! The things I learned from her,*
*When sorrow walked with me.*

## Knowledge Speaks, Wisdom Listens

A wise man was silent
As he listened for a while
An open mouth says nothing
I shall leave you with a smile

He walked away with wisdom
Not a word was said
What's the secret to serenity
It's all in your head

Listen with your heart
Never listen with your ears
Never speak too much
Because no one really hears

Whisper with compassion
Never speak out of turn
There is so much that you're missing
There is so much for you to learn

Walk with silence
Let peace be your guide
Try to be quiet
Learn peace of mind

He held my hand for a moment
Said may you find your peace
Hold your tongue with silence
Let others speak

Learn from my wisdom
Let knowledge speak
For those who listen
It's the wisdom that they seek

He looked back over his shoulder
Said you must never forget
The path that you walk down
Should never lead to regret

# 118.   Norby – June 8th 2019

Sad news. As I write, Norby (BN) is in a hospital-induced coma. It was in 1978 that myself, Dave Fairclough and Norby set sail for California. The hospital is taking him off life support at midnight, as it's only the machine that is keeping him alive. He had eye cancer that spread to his face, then to his brain, then he had kidney failure. Clinically he's brain dead as I write

He'll be in a better place soon. No more pain and suffering for him! My thoughts are with his dear family and of course his friends.

As I write I'm sitting at his bedside. Brain dead but the machine is keeping him alive. I will tell him everyone sends their love, but I don't know if he can hear me. So sad

The machines are keeping him alive. His kidneys are failing. It's just hours or a day. It's just a matter of time. So sad

And that's it. They've turned the machine off. I was with him 'till the last.

*(Karl)*

*In the winter of '77-'78 Norby, myself and a few others drove down to the Canary Islands and lived the hippie lifestyle in an old prison camp on the beach. He was good and reliable company on that trip.*

*Then in 1980, when a pal of ours, Steve Wheelband, had just come out of the Merchant Navy, and I was training Sunday mornings in Peter Faye's boxing gym, Norby suddenly turned up in The Cricketers in Bournemouth, where we used to have a drink after training. He just walked through the door, back from the States for a holiday. Over a few pints, he told us what Danny was up to and persuaded Steve and myself to head out to California. We never looked back.*

*He's in a better place now. No more pain.*

# 119.    The Story of Norby

The story of Norby - from 1977 to 2019. The story of our lives and friendship, which were conceived in Bournemouth UK.

We all met on the beaches as deckies, and we bonded immediately. There's a stretch of beach that runs the length of Bournemouth to Boscombe and further, and kids like us who'd left home headed from all over the country to the coast. Some worked in hotels, some in bars, but every lad wanted to work the deckchairs and, of course, chat up all the holiday girls

It was always a bit of a pose working the deckchairs. You were always tanned better than anybody else, that deep mahogany suntan, like wood stain, that you can only get from working all summer on the beach.

Norby, a plasterer by trade, was from up north and found friends easy. Dave Fairclough was one of his closest friends and Norby's good looks assured he was never without a girlfriend. As with all good things, the summer came to an end and the winter was brutal. At that time Freddie Laker was spreading his wings and a £99 return to California seemed the ticket for us. So it was decided. Dave, Norby and myself packed our bags and boarded for the 11-hour flight

We arrived and were greeted by the famous space ship building restaurant, and palm trees and heat. Our good looks and English accents were going to knock 'em bandy Hahahahaha.

We ended up in Inglewood, in a seedy hotel with cockroaches for friends. Norby, as calm as ever, said, "It's only for the night." We knew we'd made a mistake, but were there for ten days, so we agreed to see it through ......

# 120.   Inglewood (by Karl)

*I'm interrupting Danny's story here, just so the reader gains a proper perspective of the Inglewood area. You see the areas of South-Central Los Angeles - Watts, Compton, Inglewood and even East L.A. - are arguably the most violent in the whole of the United States. For these are the territories of the infamous Bloods and Crips.*

*In 1981, the year I was driving cab around these areas, there were over 150 gang-related homicides in South-Central L.A. alone. And by now those annual figures have more than doubled. There are wars going on there.*

*Let me make this perfectly clear. These young men of colour grow up in a war zone. It's all they know. All of their role models are either killers or wear colostomy bags. For the most part, while driving cab in South-Central, I worked Watts and Compton, but occasionally I'd work Inglewood too.*

*Inglewood, sometimes nicknamed Inglewatts, is about 75% black and 25% Mexican.*

*After Watts, Inglewood always seemed like nothing to me, but that was because I was used to Watts and Compton. There were even a few white faces about, and there are only a couple of* streets in Inglewood that are really bad. One of the drivers got robbed, another driver got beaten up and another guy had the big stick waved at him. The big stick in this case being a double-barrelled 'over-and-under.' They threatened to blow his head off.

One guy I had to pick up in Inglewood answered the door on crutches. When I inquired as to how he broke his leg, he told me he'd been shot by an O.G. from the Nine-Oh Mafia set.

The worst street in Inglewood is 102nd, between 36th and 39th. This is where the driver got robbed. I'd just radioed in "clear" outside some projects on 102nd one night when I heard a couple of bangs but thought nothing of it. However, as I started to drive off I saw a black guy running down the street with a gun in his hand. Whatever he'd been up to, I didn't want to know. I got out of there as quick as I could.

I had a lot more adventures in Watts and Compton, including having a gun shoved in my face, but seeing as Danny's only mentioned Inglewood here, that'll do for now.

(anyone interested in my life as a white cab driver in one of the most violent areas of the States can read my book 'Grit: The Banter and Brutality of the Late-Night Cab Driver').

# 121. Norby continued

After ten days, Norby, Dave and I moved to Santa Monica. We got a motel room at The Pacific Sands motel. Santa Monica was paradise. The King's Head, the most popular English pub, offered employment for me, and Norby found building work (he was a brilliant builder). Dave got a job as a jeweller, which was his trade.

We all found an apartment on 6th Street. Norby was kind and funny and women loved him. He dated a tall American chick called Wendy for a while. However, as with all of us expats, we tend to go our separate ways. Norby never left Santa Monica, and I'd see him about town from time to time. He loved golf and lived a wonderful life.

In the later years Norby had an ingrown hair in his eye and due to the cost of medical treatment over here he neglected the condition and it turned to cancer. God sent Brian a guardian angel named Rob and his lovely wife to help him gain employment. He got Norby to and from the hospital for his radiation treatment. They never left his side. They were both angles, right up until Norby's passing.

The cancer had taken Norby's eye and he wore his pirate patch and never ever complained. He laughed and was always upbeat. But the cancer came back with a vengeance, and a tumour was discovered. So again he was operated on but it had spread to his brain and the rest of his body. Never have I met a braver man. He never ever said a bad word about anyone.

Norby worked on the beach in Venice, still good looking with his trademark beard which added a kind of Bee Gees look. He was still in great shape and loved the beach life. It's been 40 years since we were all working as deckies on Bournemouth Beach.

In closing, Norby died peacefully and I'm sure he would have loved the sunny day that kissed him home.

RIP NORBY. He lived a great life.

# 122. Norby

Born of steel and iron
Stronger than a Canadian bear
Quiet as the morning rain
A shoulder that was always there

Never spoke with hatred
A heart he wore on his sleeve
And now he's left us way too soon
But today we will not grieve

We'll join him with our memories
And lest we all forget
That time belongs to all of us
Let's live without regret

I met Norby so very long ago
When youth was our best friend
Those summers in good old Bournemouth
How we hated them to end

Norby held court on the beaches
A tanned and stunning man
Girls flocked around the flicker of flame
And got burnt in the mid-day sand

A man of many emotions
He lived on his own terms
A beard that hid his desires
That girls soon quickly learned

Time past as it surly does
As a restless soul within

So we decided to leave old Bournemouth
And hope America would let us in

We boarded our morning flight
Excitement filled the air
Norby chatted up the stewardess
He admired her jet-black hair

We landed in Los Angeles
On a warm summer's day
And headed for a hotel
The boys were on their way

Never seen a vibrating bed
Or a TV that never ends
But here we are in Inglewood
We're going out to make friends

If you have never seen Inglewood
Then you won't understand
You better have a set of balls
And run as fast as you can

So we decided to leave Dodge
And I don't mean a van
I mean we're out of Inglewood
We got out as fast as we can

We ended up in Santa Monica
Paradise on our tongues
Four words we loved
Girls sea sand and sun

We all found work quite easy
Norby got a job first
Dave didn't waste anytime
As California quenched our thirst

We danced our lives away
The King's Head was our home
Ruth and Phil were the owners
And Magic Numbers got us home

After many fun-loving years
We went our separate ways
Often are my memories
With far off brighter days

We all slowly aged
And time has taken its toll
I heard the sad news
Norby hadn't long to go

I rushed to Norby's bedside
Machines were now his friends
Just a matter of time
Before my friend's life would end

Norby left us way too soon
I watched him pass away
The sun kissed Norby home
For he died on a sunny day

RIP NORBY

# 123.   Prostate

Just passing on love from my friend in Liverpool, Brian Omar, of whom Karl writes, *"I always loved Brian's eyes. I'm sure he won't mind me saying but he has the piercing eyes of Angel Eyes from The Good, The Bad and The Ugly, played by Lee Van Cleef. Great eyes!"*

We grew up with Norby on the beaches of Bournemouth in 1977. Recently Brian went to the doctor and discovered he had prostate cancer. He sought treatment and is back to normal, thank God.

So I've just had my undercarriage looked at, you know, finger job wahayyyyyy!!!!

I CANT STRESS ENOUGH TO ALL MEN; GO GET CHECKED, PLEASE LISTEN TO ME. IT TAKES TEN MINUTES AND JOB DONE

As they say, 'Finger up the bum is a job well done.'

It's a wonderful feeling that I have no cancer, at least in that dept. Get checked early, and your life will be extended. Please please lads, get checked, even your own doctor can do the bum

AND tell your sons to check their bollocks for lumps. If caught in the early stage Testicular

Cancer is ALWAYS curable. If left to the latter stages, it's nearly always fatal.

Bit of a no-brainer really.

Women, of course, don't have a prostate, but they do have a skene gland located on the anterior wall of the vagina – it's what helps keep the vagina lubricated. It's very rare for a cancer to develop here; in fact, it's only found in less than 0.003% of all female genital cancers, but women should still be checked.

Men can get breast cancer, of course, with 500 men a year dying from this particular cancer. But generally speaking men are at a much higher risk of contracting prostate cancer, and women breast cancer in women.

This piece was written in honour of Brian Omar and to awareness of his own battle, but of course EVERYONE SHOULD BE SCREENED FOR ALL SORTS OF CANCERS. Google the symptoms and if anything concerns you take it straight to the doctor

Get checked. All of us want to check out in our own time

Love ya

*(Karl)*

*A month or two after Danny penned the above I had the honour of attending a fundraiser for Prostate Cancer organised by Brian Omar in Liverpool. We arrived late (and scruffy, thanks to coming straight from football) but nobody seemed to mind. Brian had organised a raffle, karaoke and two bars. All in all, over £1200 was raised that night alone!*

*An extremely worthy cause, and it was terrific to catch up on some old memories of the beach days Danny speaks about and, of course, some of the mischief we all got up to. As Danny says, we could all well have ended up in prison.*

*And one of my best mates in the world, Laine, was there too. I always give Laine huge hugs and hold hands all night. She's like a sister to me. My wife, Sue, always says, "The pair of you, just get a bloody room will you," but she's only kidding, she knows our love is purely platonic.*

*We don't get up to Liverpool much, but it was great to see Laine, her family and Brian*

# 124.    27 Years

As the world turns, 27 years of marriage, ups and downs, deaths, illness, sadness, and we're still fighting to be together. I defy any couple to live together without a few bumps in the road. We've had plenty. I see the world square, she sees it round. I see a glass of wine, she sees a bottle. I see going out on my motorbike, and she sees laying on the beach in far-off exotic lands, an island preferably with a cocktail in her hand. And don't get me started with toilet seats, wet towels and laundry, and toothpaste caps, but we're still together playing Happy Families. Kids grown and flown the nest and there's just the two of us. She's watching all the stupid Kardashian shows and Orange County Wives and I'm watching the history channel.

She sees couples on Facebook in far away paradise places and says, "Let's go to the Turks and Caicos Islands in the Caribbean. We end up in Palm Springs.

You see, we compromise, but through it all I'm right by her side and that's love. She sometimes stares at me in the darkness of the night and I know what's on her mind; "Of all the men I could have married, I'm stuck with him."

I really think she should work for the unemployment office because when I'm not working, she finds things for me to do around the house. She is my world, my rock, and if you catch her on a good day, she makes my life wonderful. However, if the nails come out, you'll find me sleeping in my truck.

She loves her toast and egg in the morning, and a tea, and then her day starts by saying, "Are you working today because I want you out of the house?"

I tend to lie and get out of her way. But as I hope you can read by this piece, laughter still holds our marriage together ….. I think.

And if you get Colette to laugh it makes for a great marriage. 27 years and still hanging on in.

So Colette, here's to another 27 years of torture, fights, shouting, slamming doors and making up. Marriage; the truth, the whole and nothing but the truth. I love you, Colette.

## 125. For All Fantastic Dads (on Father's Day)

Laughter filled the bedrooms
Screaming and crying too
The house is full running kids
What's a dad to do

Becky is the fastest
Susan hates to take a bath
And Michael is the funniest
He makes everybody laugh

The wonder of a child's face
The tears that break your heart
They grow so fast before your eyes
Suddenly you're all apart

They leave home as all children do
They find their wings and fly
And parents watch them drive away
As you wave them all goodbye

Sometimes there's a phone call
Sorry dad, I have to run
And tears run down your face
Make sure to say hello to mum

Christmas in an empty home
Just pictures share your joy
Only seemed like yesterday
When Michael was a little boy

Now Susan works in Texas

Becky lives in Spain
And Michael joined the navy
And we all live in pain

I gaze out to our garden
The swing still cries alone
She often moves in windswept days
When are the kids coming home?

The slide still holds my memories
The screams of children's play
And parties in the garden
How time slipped slowly away

Tomorrow is never promised
The children have now all grown
Empty bedrooms never sleep
They too hate being alone

So on this special Father's Day
Reflect on what you have
Take a long look in the mirror
And remember you're a fantastic Dad

## 126. Goodbye Doesn't Last Forever

Every year I'm reminded
The footsteps you left behind
Your shoes were too big to fill
How life can be so unkind

I held your hand for the very last time
Saw you take your last breath
Memories flood like the rushing tide
I'm drowning with regret

I left home as child
The world was at my feet
Thought you would live forever
Thought life was oh so sweet

But time took you from me
My world fell apart
How am I to carry on
With a broken heart

Rain fell this morning
It helped to hide my tears
Days have turned to weeks
Those weeks have turned to years

I miss you more than ever, Dad
The nights dance your smile
I know that we will meet again
I know it may take a while

I kiss the sky each morning
I know Mum's by your side

Tell her that I love her too
For this is not goodbye

# 127.   Beds are for Flowers

I'm older than yesterday
And wiser by the day
I made mistakes like all of us
But there's a price to pay

I laughed away the hours
When time was on my side
And now tomorrow found me
And left my youth behind

I wasted precious moments
And stayed in bed all day
I slept like a baby
And dreamed my life away

Now that I am older
And my legs have passed me by
My back aches each morning
As my tears watch me cry

My eyes don't see clearly
The mirror is not my friend
My doctor makes empty promises
And says I'm on the mend

And yes, I ate from the Tree of Life
But alas I didn't chew
Regrets I carry day after day
Because I still have lots to do

The sun had been waiting
The rain was at my door
Fields and forest were a moment away

Ready for me to explore

So there's a moral to my poem
It's a story of your bed
Pull back those fucking covers
Before they find you dead

## 128. Slave to the Needle

She speaks without a whisper
She cries nor with pain
She laughs away the hours
And dances the night away

She cuts you with her lipstick
She licks you while you bleed
Don't be fooled by her beauty
Her habit has a need

Her lips can sink many hearts
Her tears can fill a pool
Never turn your back on her
Don't take her for a fool

Late at night, in the midnight hour
She tiptoes across the floor
She slips away into the night
She's done this many time before

Drugs are her best friend
No lover need apply
Loneliness follows her everywhere
So many times she's cried

A cocktail and a phone call
Her makeup covered smile
She left in such a hurry
Said she'll be back in a while

And that's where they found her
Needle by her side
Lying in a doorway

This is where she died

No funeral, just raindrops
No mourners by the grave
A victim to the needle
And she became the slave

## 129.   This is What I Have to Deal With (almost all the time)

Customer;          Hi, can you lay a concrete path?

Me;                Yes, no problem

Customer;          Can you give me a price?

Me;                Yes of course

Customer;          Can you start right away?

Me;                Yes no problem

Customer;          Great job. In fact, it's just what I want. Can you call next week, I will pay you?

Me;                Yes of course


Two weeks later;        RING RING no answer

Three weeks later;      RING RING no answer

Four weeks later;       RING RING RING RING

Customer;          Oh hi, the cheque has to be sent from corporate office. Should take a week or so

Me;                Mmmmm okay

Six weeks later;        RING RING RING RING Hi, the check has not arrived

Customer;          Really! Let me track it down and get back to you

Seven weeks later;      RING RING RING no answer


So I leave a message; Hi, this is Danny. In the morning, I'll be coming round and I'll be smashing out the fucking concrete path I laid

RING RING RING;         Hi Danny, can you come and pick up your check today

Grrrrrrrrrrrrrrrrrr

Its hell. They play the game. I know I should get up-front money, but I try the friendly approach and use my own money, just in case they think I'm not coming back. It's a bloody shame to deal with the pain. Try and order a cup of coffee and then say to the coffee shop owner, "I'll pay you next month." See what he says

I honestly get it all the time. It's the only trade you have to wait to be paid. Can you hang a door? Yes, no problem. All done, looks great. My husband's not here to pay you, can you come back? Oh okay, when shall I come back? Well, he's at work at the moment. Oh, okay. I'll have him call you. Oh okay thanks

NO CALL

RING RING;                    Sorry he's not here at the moment

I actually end up grovelling at the very same door I just hung

Grrrrrrrrrrrrrrr

# 130.   Life of a Handyman

Hello, Is this Dan
Yes, how are you tonight
I'm fine, what's your problem
My switch broke to my light

Okay, I'm on my way over
And I fixed it right away
We chatted for a while
And I waited to be paid

How much do I owe you
Just a hundred for a service call
He said, I'm sorry I don't have it
And left me waiting in the hall

He said I'll give you twenty dollars
That's all the money I have
A Rolls Royce in his driveway
Made me feel bloody mad

I said I'll take a cheque
I don't mind at all
Once again, he went away
And made me feel a fool

Look take the twenty dollars
I have more work to pass your way
I stand before you a broken man
Because I took it anyway

This is what I deal with
Day after day
You work your arse to the bone
And then you wait to get paid

I got a call to lay concrete
A job that was in my heart
We shook hands on an agreement
She said, When can you start?

Never worked so hard in heat
I got the concrete laid
She smiled with the completion
I said when do I get paid

Oh, came the cries of wonderment
Your work came out great
The office is closed at the moment
I'm afraid it's getting late

Can you come back tomorrow?
Of course, I said with a smile
The next day she kept me waiting
The cheque may take awhile

Look, I spent all my money on material
I need my money today
I could see she was not budging
So I had to walk away

Six weeks of waiting
Just as my concrete's getting hard
The amount of work I did
Repairing her bloody yard

I'm venting my rage and anger
Just to try and get paid
Trust me when I tell you
I face this every bloody day

*A handyman is a provider when you require a job done quickly and a parasite when he asks for payment.*

# 131. Neurosis - For those who don't understand

For those who don't understand, and I appreciate that's a lot of people, I'm trying to use the pages of this book – interspersed with my at times chaotic poetry (which is often my only way of dealing with the world) - to try and explain anxiety, depression and neurosis, and I'm not too sure I'm doing such a great job (I guess the book reviews will tell hahahahahaha). It's not easy to put into words just how a neurotic is feeling. GOD, I HATE LABELS.

You see, I think that no one wants to be burdened with my issues because they've all got their own issues to deal with. I know this can be frustrating to hear when you are genuinely trying to help, but for me it's like having one foot on the throttle and one foot on the brake. The throttle's telling me to "Go fast! Go fast! Go fast!" And so I start spinning my wheels, but because the brake pedal is pressed down at the same time, my brake shoes or pads or whatever you call them inside my brain try and stop my wheels from turning. Inside I can feel all this friction and something's telling me, "Hey dickhead, we ain't going nowhere today!"

Because the energy produced by my throttle and the power it sends to my so-called transmission –

whose job it is to make sure that the right amount of power goes to my body to 'drive' it at a given speed - is fighting the brake components, it causes burnouts. As my brakes are trying stop me moving, the kinetic energy in my brain causes heat energy to build on all my components, causing metaphorical smoke to come out of me at a subconscious level. Burnout!

Does that make sense?

Didn't think so.

You see, you can prevent the burnout by taking your feet off the pedals. YOU can do that, but for ME, it isn't that easy.

I'm more like Zebedee on the Magic Roundabout, a talking, out-of-control, jack-in-the-box with magical powers who's always springing off the roundabout of my mind, with my boss-eyes focused, a little too lustfully, it must be said, on Florence. Boing!

I'm not crazy at all.

You see, there's not always a reason for a bad day. There are days when I wake up and it's noisy in my head for no rational reason whatsoever. Ask me to clarify why and you're trying to find a logical reason. I know you mean well, but sometimes there isn't a reason. That doesn't, however, negate from the fact that my own experience is any less real or impossible to deal with.

Imagine yourself on holiday. You don't speak the language and you can't read menus in restaurants. Normally it's not a problem because you expect everyone else to speak English, and they do. But imagine going to Xisha in the South China Seas where everyone speaks either Hoàng Sa or Cát Vàng. Your senses are going to be overwhelmed attempting to absorb all the bizarre and unfamiliar sounds. You're simply not on the same wavelength as anyone else. Now imagine that you're in a place you're familiar with, but all of the above still applies. Without warning, nothing is recognizable.

That's what it's like. It sucks

There's a constant battle going on inside of me between wanting to engage in life with all my heart and soul and wanting to bolt like a rabbit back to my burrow. I can hide it for a while, but it is a struggle. It's not because the person trying to help is boring, far from it, or that they've done something wrong. I'm just so fucking tired, and maybe, just maybe, I don't want to do any more magic tricks or tell any more jokes or make up any more stupid poems. But I can't tell you that

I know that makes me sound like a dick, and I know you try to understand, but what works with me one day might not help the next, so I'm all lopsided in my head, which is why I've chosen this book to illustrate how my thoughts jump about all the time. Karl and I could have 'edited' it better, but we chose not to in order to expose how my thinking bounces about without rhyme nor reason. So I rabbit away about anxiety and depression and suicide and then I write a poem, but the poetry is my way of clearing my head.

And yet I don't know how to tell you that without confusing you or turning you away. Sometimes I just want to be left alone. I know they say to talk to those suffering from anxiety or depression – I know I'm the one who says that - but sometimes we just want to be left alone. What kind of sense does that make! None! So it's easier just to say "I'm fine."

At least you are still putting up with me, offering support, and that alone means so much. Somebody cares. But sometimes I just want to be left alone. And next week I may need a hug so bad it hurts.

The trouble, if I'm really honest, is that I don't want to hurt you. You see, I can't shake the feeling that if I confide in you, one of us in going to get hurt, so just to protect YOU I choose not to share what's in my head. Because if you get hurt I'll look at the damage and say "I did this."

Guilt plagues me all the time; because I rebelled and ate the forbidden   fruit.

I feel incredibly guilty about being too hard to deal with or being a burden on the people I love. And that's when suicidal thoughts come in. When things aren't great, I hurt, and I don't want you to hurt as well.

I know none of this makes sense – or maybe it does – but I tell you something; whatever tomorrow brings ……... bring that fucker on!

## 132.    So if I hate labels …..

Why did I call myself neurotic in the last chapter?

Because I keep running 'worst-case scenarios' over and over again in my mind on a loop, and I exist in an anxious emotional state most of the time. And if that isn't neurosis I don't know what is.

However, I do try and keep it all in perspective and maintain a healthy sense of humour.

It's a myth, by the way, that happy people have a better sense of humour than people who are more serious. However, on the other side of the coin, a good sense of humour can certainly go a long way towards keeping a person cheerful. And in that respect humour can definitely be a stress-coping mechanism. It can be an amazing line of defence.

A sense of humour is now viewed by psychologists - who are now learning to respect laughter - as a 'character strength.' Now I'm hardly a neuroscientist – I'm a DJ who does a little bit of handyman work on the side – so I Googled it. It turns out that a character strength that lifts us above, or helps us go beyond, normal behaviour is termed Transcendence, and the five top Transcendences are appreciation of beauty, gratitude, optimism (or even simply hope), spirituality and yes, humour. And I get that. All of us, especially us neurotics, take life far too seriously, which is why at times in this book I've been a little light-hearted. It's not meant to be disrespectful to others going through their own mental health issues, and I hope it isn't taken that way. It's just that I believe the ability to laugh about a situation will not only make my own life easier, but by spreading a bit of fun, I hope it helps others too.

The downside to this, of course, is that people expect me to be funny all the time, and I can't.

But enough about humour. As that great philosopher, Mark Twain, once said, "Studying humour is like dissecting a frog. You may learn a lot but all you end up with is a dead frog."

To be neurotic means that you are anxious and depressed, and for these reasons, you can't function at 100%. It's not psychotic. Psychotics are a pain in the arse. They can be extremely volatile. I'm not. And, although I've had my moments in the past, I rarely engage in what society would call highly deviant or socially unacceptable behaviour.

You can, of course, have those who suffer from psychotic depressive disorder. Do you see why I hate labels? PDD is like major depression except those who suffer from it can also suffer hallucinations and delusions and hear voices. The psychotic is out of touch with reality, and although I run worst-case scenarios repeatedly in my head I am, I like to think, fairly grounded.

The psychotic depressives have realised that their thoughts are not 'right' so for the most part they keep them to themselves. You never really know if they're peaceful and reticent because they don't have a lot to say or what they do have to say is so abhorrent that they really shouldn't be sending it out into the universe.

And it's probably best not to find out.

A sociopath, for instance, is psychotic (as well as narcissistic), just that they hide it better. Sociopaths can actually be very charming, you know, but they're evil.

The neurotic, however, has a tendency towards anxiety, depression, self-doubt and even shyness. If you knew me you wouldn't think that because I'm a DJ, but being a DJ is my comfort blanket and, as such, I can get away with wearing my neurosis or anxiety as a badge of honour. Away from my DJ stand, however, I'm just me; anxious, afraid, apprehensive, distressed and fearful. I'm a fucking basket case!

How's that for a label?

## 133. Anxiety and worry and all that neurotic stuff

It's apparently quite normal. So once again allow me to try and help as best I can.

When you're young the dance of life is at your feet and time doesn't exist. In fact, we all look forward to the next birthday. Although having said that time does play with your health and, of course, the death of parents, family and friends add to the mix. The sun waits and the rain pours, and the days just go on and on, and you, of course, go along for the ride.

As you age you find grey hairs and wrinkles, your sex drive slows down and, of course, aches and pains and tiredness, and that is the ageing process. Some people stay fit, up at four a.m. for a swim or a run and, of course, they eat well and they look as sick as fuck hahahahhahaha

Just joking

Back to anxiety (as this is why you bought the book, and I've got to give you value for money). Anxiety can hit at any age and it attacks any gender. But it loves depression. It feeds on worry. It comes out of nowhere. I've noticed young adults suffering in silence.

Without mentioning any names, a lovely lad was in hospital with high pulse rate, high blood pressure and palpitations. Turns out it was nothing. When I say nothing, I mean no serious condition. But the seed has been sown. Anxiety starts to fester and if not worked on it will work on you.

Who would think Danny the DJ, the funny man, the clown, the idiot would be affected by its claws?

I'm not happy to have it, but I'm happy to help others who hide and, on a day-by-day basis crumble.

Psychic tension can destroy you. It can humble you to the core. People who know me think, "How does Danny manage to be so happy?" It's because I hide behind my mask. My 'clown' mask. There are so many people who talk to me and ask questions and I can see they're suffering. Most of my family walk in my shoes. It's so common it makes you sick. The world we live in has no safety net. It's moves too fast and you'd better have your rent paid, bills paid, and most of all be healthy. Those are the cold bloody facts. Anxiety will put you in hospital, and it's a vicious circle

Here are the symptoms;

   1) Thoughts that are wild

2) Financial concerns, worries about bills
3) Health worry
4) Age worry
5) Work worry
6) Etc.

The adrenaline kicks in and the party is on. I'm getting anxiety writing this, yet I want all who read it to understand that it's very, very common

And so, the answer to the age-old question; what is going on in my brain? Research is on its way to uncover triggers that bring on an episode of anxiety. I've personally found that distraction is the key. If you're feeling strange or panicky it's adrenaline that is bursting out of your brain. It needs an outlet. So head phones on, music on and go for a jog or a walk or read a book. Play anxiety at its own game. It hates to be ignored.

I truly hope that somewhere in this book there are a few lines that will help. You can contact me anytime. I'm up all night fighting my demons. Some nights I win, some nights they won't let me sleep. But I'm learning, very gradually, how to deal with my anxiety

Love ya

## 134. George in the Hole (by Karl)

George went out for a stroll
While he was out he fell in a hole
And try as he would he couldn't get out.
To fall in the hole wasn't his choice
He called for help at the top of his voice
But his rescue he started to doubt

Along came a man full of muscles
Laughing he threw him a shovel
Man up, you loser, dig deep.
George dug that hole deeper and deeper
He swore he'd soon meet the Grim Reaper
And he dug, and he climbed, and he leaped

A neighbour was next to come walking along
Listen to me, you've got to stay strong
I'll be happy to give some advice.
Use the shovel that first man gave you
That's all you need to save you
Put in some effort, that should suffice

George used his tools
And followed the rules
And dug the hole deeper still.
Along came a doctor
And as soon as he clocked her
She said, Here I'll give you a pill

Well, the pills went to his brain
And he forgot about the pain
But he was still in the hole when they ran out.

He called for assistance
His very existence
Was nowhere he wanted to hang out

Along came a psychiatrist
Who spoke the quietest
And who asked a lot of questions.
How did you get down there?
Did you once have long hair?
But offered no suggestions

Tell me about your parents
Do you like your appearance?
Do you suffer from a sense of loss?
Do you feel lonely?
You know you're not the only
person who hates his boss

George thanked the psychiatrist
For coming along to assist
But he was still in the hole when he left.
He cried out aloud
And drew a big crowd
But no one seemed that impressed

Then along came a friend
Who began to descend
Down into the hole with George.
George started to panic
His brain, it went manic
He felt he was going through the wars

Now there's two of us stuck down here
We're both going to disappear
You'd have been more help up there.
Brother, he said, relax
I won't let you slip through the cracks

I'm not going to leave, I swear

For I've been here before
No need to implore
I know how to get out of the hole.
I'll stay with you
'till you're not so blue
Together we'll let no one control

You see, it's okay to be a little screwed up in the
head
It doesn't mean you're losing the thread
And it doesn't mean you have to stay in this pit.
It's only those who are screwed up in the heart
They're really the ones who are falling apart
And they're the ones who are a piece of shit

I know your brain feels like a cyclone
But with friends you're never alone
We've got a smile to give you.
Just make the request
For we've never left
Even if we have to jump in the hole with you

When someone is going through a tough time, just sit there with them. No preaching. Those horrible little shits who spend their whole life preaching at people, making out they're some kind of guru, will never understand that sometimes a person who's hurting just wants you to crack open a beer and 'be with them.'

Talking isn't necessary. If someone won't come out into the light, then go into the darkness with them and sit there until they're ready.

They don't want to hear what that horrible little shit imagines are 'clever' words anyway. They don't want advice. And they certainly don't want to be preached at.

They just want to know you're there.

Sometimes, it really is as simple as that

(by Karl)

# 135.    There are no answers

There are no answers. Just questions. What happens to me? Where do these feelings come from? How come now?

The answers are a mystery. The brain won't let you think for yourself. It's so complex that there are no answers except worry about growing old, hope you have enough money, hope you're not lonely, hope you don't suffer and hope you can take a shit. Don't tell me that's nothing to worry about. Don't make laugh

Don't hide suicide

# 136.   Decisions (by Karl)

*I recently attended a course that is a regular in the construction industry. It's a five-day course followed by a two-day refresher every five years. It's a walk in the park really, but since I last attended (five years ago) they've added a section on Mental Health to the syllabus, which is all to the good, of course.*

*I've published a 12-page newsletter on Mental Health in the Construction Industry, and I've spoken to 300-400 construction workers on the subject before allowing them out on site.*

*However, when we came to this section on the course, a geezer at the back said, "Oh, here we go, this shit again."*

*But before I could say anything to shut the twat up this big old boy sitting quite close to him – we were all seated in a U-shape as is common for these workshops – said, "Well, hold on a minute. You don't want to be so quick to judge."*

*And he told us his story. He said that just a few weeks ago he woke up in the middle of the night and thought he'd get himself a cup of tea. He went downstairs and boiled the kettle. But then he thought maybe he fancied a coffee. So he put the tea bag back in its little cannister and spooned some coffee into the cup. But then he* wasn't too sure. Did he want tea or coffee. This went round and round in his head, he boiled the kettle half a dozen times, until he ended up in tears.

He couldn't even decide if he wanted tea or coffee. "What fucking use am I if I can't make a decision like that?"

The next day he was coming home from work, standing on the Tube station platform and he started thinking, "I could throw myself in front of this train. There's no reason why I shouldn't. Who'd miss me. I'm no fucking use at all. I can't even decide whether to make a cup of tea or a cup of coffee. And now I can't decide whether to throw myself in front of this train. I don't what to do. Shall I jump in front of the train .... Or not?"

The room was silent.

"You see, mate," he went on. "It's cunts like you that make me think I should have thrown myself under that train. Because what you don't understand, what you'll never understand, is that the decision to throw myself under a train, or not, carries no more importance to me as the decision whether to have a coffee or a tea. It's all the same to me. Do you get that? It's the same decision.

"No, I don't suppose you get that at all, do you?

"But to me it's the same decision."

# 137. I'm on that road to nowhere

I just exist

And I'm very lucky to have the front row seat to the greatest show on earth, but I just want to be normal again. However, after seeing so many deaths it's a wakeup call to life. I'm petrified that I will have something wrong with me. I wait like an expectant mother, it's bloody insane. Any ailment and I'm at the hospital. I'm like a gerbil on a wheel, but I take one moment at a time and breathe

Thank God I can breathe

# 138. Bloody anxiety is running the show

It's a nightmare, it's a constant reminder of life and the worry of the future. I didn't sign up for this. Now my son has chosen a dangerous occupation and so I don't sleep with worry.

The brain wants to dance, then the door opens and all the brain's friends want in and then the DJ turns up and the brain is flying and always the girl that wants just one more song is a pest and the DJ shuts the music down, and the doorman throws everybody out and then the lights go out, and you're all alone. But then the heart wants to reopen the club and starts beating faster and bangs on the door, then Xanax Police calm it down and finally a moment of rest until heart and brain get a second wind

Welcome to my world of anxiety. Good job I'm not a whack job hahahahaha

I'm trying. I'm really trying. But my son wanted to live a life of a danger, so I have to step aside and support him

It's hell, but workable. I don't take meds anymore and I'm fighting every day. It's very common, this condition, and behind closed doors the silent suffer. But I'm not the silent one. I speak out for help. It's debilitating but, as I say, one day at a time.

## 139.   Party for my Brain

Decided to throw a party
Invited all my problems along
Laughter was in the corner
Singing a silly song

Stupid was talking to Angry
As Psycho raised his voice
Then Wisdom intervened
And Decision made a choice

Problem stood in the doorway
Talking to a fool
Asshole started laughing
As Passive kept his cool

Pride made way for Bigot
As Racist spoke his mind
Decency stepped in
And said, 'Colour is just blind.'

Everyone was drinking
And the booze started to flow
Shut-Up started laughing
Told Stupid where to go

Then the door flew open
Malice just walked in
Sensible tried talking
But problem's just begin

Everyone was shouting
As laughter filled the room

Passion grabbed hold of Wisdom
They decided to get a room

Everyone was leaving
Cause they couldn't get along
Common Sense prevailed
And Trouble was all gone

All that's left is Silence
As the night draws to an end
Out of all my problems
Silence is my best friend

# 140.    A Puppy's Tale

She was born on the streets
With nothing to eat
Her eyes blue as the sky
And there she laid
And no one prayed
For the puppy who was about to die

Two men in a truck
Saw the pup
She was cold from the morning dew
Fleas and disease
They thought she would freeze
They picked her up and gave her something to
chew

She shook like a bush
And by the looks
Her eyes were fading away
But she wagged her tail
And you could tell
She was fighting the rest of the way

Her days were spent in a shelter
Looking through the bars of hell
She just sat in a corner
Waiting to get out of jail

She would often walk to the wire
And hope her time would come
But at the end of the day
There she laid
The puppy was the lonely one

Sunday in the shelter
Children came to play
Sally walked by the cage
And decided she wanted to stay

Sally sat with the puppy
As tears fell from her face
I want to take her home with me
And get her out of this place

The cage door was opened
The puppy was finally free
Sally was dancing down the hall
She's coming home with me

What shall we call her?
As they walked to the car
Sally thought for a moment
And said, I'm calling her Star

Star, said her mother
As the puppy sat on her knee
I'm calling her Star
So she can always watch over me

Please adopt from a shelter; Danny

# 141.   Time to let go

Held her for the first time
My angel to my chest
Fleeting moments passed us by
As a father, I did my best

I thought summers would last forever
Alas they went so fast
She smiles through her innocence
And time has slipped my grasp

Makeup and lipstick
Replaced her broken toys
Her youthful laughter echoes
Now she's talking to young boys

Time has come to let her go
And see her live her life
As lonely as a father gets
She will one day be a wife

And memories run with floods of tears
My baby lost to time
I hold those moments in my heart
A child that once was mine

An empty bedroom awaits me
A door that opens wide
I can still recall her laughter
When Kerrie would run and hide

The silence wakes my shadows
Here stands a broken man
It's time to let my baby fly
And time to let go of her hand

# 142.   Do it Now

Don't think of tomorrow as just another day
It's you future and it's slipping away
The tides of the sea always kiss the shore
Time is in your hands, there is no time for more

Children are like flowers, they blossom as they
grow
Fathers and mothers watch their children go
We all take a turn and leave it far too late
Laughing at the future, trying to make it wait

Many idle hours
Dreaming in your bed
All the while hiding
From what lies ahead

The rush of windswept mountains
The skies that soar with heights
The seas of many colours
The magic of the night

When age taps your shoulder
And your back begins to break
Regrets and sorrow they are
All of your mistakes

The world is at your doorstep
The sun will wash your face
Looking over your shoulder
Getting back into the race

Your mirror sees the future
Don't wait for age to come

Throw away your problems
Go out and have some fun

And in your final hour
When your body has done its best
Just remember that old flower
That bloomed above the rest

# 143.   Time we Have

Wasted are the hours
Voyages not taken
Sleepless nights weeping
Tomorrow has not wakened

Water falls to bathe your heart
Let time tiptoe very slow
Sail through life's mistakes
Watch your problems flow

Seek snow-covered mountains
Let the taste of rain wash your tongue
And through the darkness of nights
Be forever young

Climb where there are hillsides
Swim in the open seas
Spread your wings far and wide
Fly upon God's breeze

Fear not the hands of time
Let laughter be your guide
Stroll with a light in your heart
Take sadness in your stride

Let not slumber chain your bed
Run through fields of grass
Rest a while to smell the world
So true it shall not last

All shall live but many not lived
So few shall kiss the stars

So many live in cages
It's time to remove those bars

Seek what fortunes awaits you
Treasures of sheer delight
Find happiness in people's hearts
Help others with their plight

Tomorrow awaits your smile
Dance to a different tune
Life is but a fleeting moment
Don't let it pass too soon

# 144. A person can be just sitting there ....

I've repeated this several times in this book, only because I'm trying to get the message across, but you'd never know. A person can be sitting there with a cyclone going on inside their head – "How can I pay my debts? Are people laughing at me? Why can't I sleep? Did I leave the oven on? Are those people looking at me? Are they going to speak to me? Are they NOT going to speak to me? Should I say something witty? I hope they don't make eye contact. If I don't speak, then they won't know I'm here. But if they do speak to me, will I say something wrong and will they get annoyed with me? Should I enter? Should I wait? How many people will be in there? Will they all look at me? Will they judge me? Are the kids going to die? I can't take it anymore. Why do these irrational thoughts ambush me? I feel like I'm drowning? I can't drown in the street, can I? You hear about people drowning in a hospital bed, don't you? A few hours after being pulled out of a river or swimming pool. Dry drowning? Am I dry drowning now? I haven't been in a river. But maybe I swallowed water in the shower. Or something. Why do I feel like I'm drowning. I should have stayed in bed. Is my heart going to jump through my chest? Am I going to trip or do something stupid? My mind never shuts up. Why do I feel so scared? I'm not normal"

That person would sit there quietly and when you ask how they are, they'll tell you, "Fine."

It's easier that way

But they're not fine, of course. They're fighting a battle you know nothing about. If they're quiet or remote they could be overthinking, or about to lose it completely, or about to have a breakdown, or sobbing inside, or they could just need a hug …. Or all of the above.

Five thousand years ago, all you had to worry about was keeping an eye out for lions and dinosaurs. And you were good at it. But now ……

# 145. What NOT to say to someone suffering from anxiety

- Come on now, things can't be all that bad
- What have you got to be anxious about?
- It's all in your head
- Have you tried meditation?
- You've got nothing to worry about
- Stop being so dramatic
- Life's too short to be sad
- Read a book on it, I'm sure that'll give good advice
- Grow some balls
- Come on, it's easy
- Why don't you throw a party?
- You only get anxiety by worrying about the future
- You don't look like you're anxious
- Everyone gets anxious from time to time, don't make such a fuss about it
- You seem so confident, are you sure you have anxiety?
- Can't you just try harder
- Move on from it
- Why can't you just cheer up?
- Just relax
- Just calm down
- Just deal with it
- Just take a few deep breaths
- Just have some confidence in yourself

- Just,  just,  just,  just,  just, justjustjustjustJUSTJUST!!!!

You have no idea how much money I would willingly pay to never hear those phrases again.

So if someone shares a confidence with you about personal things such as their struggle with desperation or despair or worry, tension or their misery, please don't be a shitty person and belittle it just because you've never experienced it. Don't brush it off. That's a shitty thing to do. You're the one person they thought they could depend on and you've now let them down. Don't do that.

Remember, even if the perceived threat isn't real, what that person is experiencing is

Just let them know you're with them, and you're going to get through this together.

# 146.    Thoughts of Suicide

I never intended to be open about my private issues, but I thought, well 'a problem shared, is half a problem' right? Never did I think I would suffer so much pain with anxiety. It cripples you. This world can be so cruel. Loneliness creeps in and then the panic. Life is frightening. So I told people, and hoped they would listen to me and help me. And in doing so it has helped me no end

And so I shared my thoughts and feelings.

I'm one moment away from hanging myself, one moment away from running screaming out into the street and throwing myself under a truck, but I know how stupid that is.

It's just a cry for help and all I need is a hug or a kind word.

## 147. He Smiled

The look in his eyes
Said it all
In God's country
He answered the call

A moment turned to tears
He smiled to the applause
Behind his smile
They open the doors

There stood his mother
Broken and proud
She fell into his arms
Along with the crowd.

Whispers went silent
Faded to cheers
Here stands her boy
He's Been away for years

Time has come
To bring him home
A mother's heart
Now she's not alone

We hold this moment
In the palm of our hands
From our boy
He's now a man

She stands by the door
And waves her boy goodbye

She trying so hard
Not to let him see her cry

He looked over his shoulder
Said he'd be back in a while
Now he's in Florida
But left us with his smile

Love Dad and Mum to our son

## 148.   No one sees him

Early morning coffee
Waiting for the train
There sits the old man
You can see the smile of pain

Platform two arriving
No one seems to care
He's used to the looks he gets
And the rage of their stare

Yesterday's newspaper
A pillow for his head
Many step over him
Not knowing if he's dead

After a long day at work
I decided to spend some time
I sat beside the saddest man
To share a bottle of wine

I tapped him on the shoulder
Said can we chat a while?
Sunlight bathed his deep blue eyes
Sadness was his smile

What is your story
To live on the street?
I went away to war
And a mine took my feet

I worked and raised a family
Then all the mills closed down
My wife took my children

She too left town

Desperation and alcohol
Became my two best friends
Life became a shadow
How I wish that it would end

I found myself alone
Washed my problems with a drink
When night time tucks me in
I'm too tired to think

I'm lost inside myself
Nothing matters anymore
I hope tomorrow never finds me
My nightmares are of the war

So that's my story
As he sipped his life away
I slipped him a twenty
I'm sorry I couldn't stay

Winter came to London
As did cold sleet and snow
What stuck in my mind
Was where did my friend go

The porter blew his whistle
As I mentioned my friend's name
Oh, said the porter
He was killed by a train

They found him on the railway lines
A letter by his side
It was addressed to his children
Said sorry for his suicide

He was buried in a far off corner
No flowers for his grave
The service for his country
And the sacrifices he made

I took him some flowers
And said my last farewell
No marker, just a number
For a man who went through hell

Here lies Sergeant Dixon
Asleep in his grave
Thank you for your service
A man who could have been saved

## Altzeimers

She sat in the hallway
Gazing off into space
Holding onto a photograph
Not knowing of his face

She was a ballerina
When she was twenty-one
Danced in the theatres
Many contests she won

She travelled the world
Met her husband on the way
Had five children
One of them passed away

She settled down in Devon
Bought a house on the coast

Of all the things she missed
Dancing was the most

Fred was her husband
Always by her side
They danced the night together
But her illness she couldn't hide

It was early in the morning
Fred sensed something was wrong
She couldn't remember
The words to her favourite song

June was slowly leaving Fred
As Alzheimer's moved her out
Memories of their love
Was never in any doubt

Fred stayed by June's side
Until the day she died
She was his soul mate
As Fred started to cry

The doctor called Fred to her bedside
He said that she can hear
He told her that he loved her
And will always be here

Her eyes slowly opened
He could swear that she said 'Fred'
He kissed her on the lips
His lovely June was dead

I curse Alzheimer's
And the price we have to pay
When you lose your loved ones
And watch their mind drift away

I swim in life, I drown in debt
The more I swim
The deeper I get
The waves cover me
With problems and debt

The sharks need feeding
And I'm their bait
Bills have to be paid
And they won't wait

I try my hardest
To stay afloat
I just need a raft
Or even a boat

I tread water
Night and day
But there's no keeping
The sharks away

Up ahead
I see dry land
I sink my feet
In the midday sand

And those of you
Who can paddle or laugh
Just be thankful
You have your raft

I rest awhile
To catch my breath
Sink or swim
I'm still in debt

# 149.  Murder

On 17<sup>th</sup> August 2018, an evil lunatic, without thinking about the consequences, picked up and held in his hand the ultimate consequence. He took the life of my best friend

You can't go from zero to 1000mph in a micro-second ….. and STAY THERE, and still be normal. This is Flashpoint Anger and this level of savagery in an attack is nearly always of a personal nature. Whatever was going on in his brain was psychotic.

He attacked Chalky with rage *after* he died. Chalky is helpless. He can't even resist him because he's dead. But to him it doesn't matter. He is completely out of control of his emotions. He's having a psychotic episode. The problem is that he's armed! He had a hammer in his hand, and he now has a knife in both hands, and he's not going to stop.

Chalky's family and friends are affected for the rest of their lives. There are no winners in this. There are only losers. And that is tragic.

Can you tell me you'll never meet a guy like this?
No. But let's hope you don't.

# 150.    (by Dave the Boxer)

The trial started in September 2019, and was adjourned until a later date as he pleaded guilty to Manslaughter by Reason of Diminished Responsibility.

Later in the month, Dave the Boxer posted online, *"A positive start to the day and an element of confidence that Chalkie's vicious murder would be avenged in that the perpetrator would be handed a sentence fitting this most brutal of crimes.*

*"WRONG!!*

*"The murderer had at the first hearing pleaded Guilty to Chalkie's manslaughter on the grounds of diminished responsibility.*

*"We, that is, his wife and all of the family and friends, believed that the Judge had somehow seen through that plea as an obvious attempt to reduce the sentence, so you can understand why we were in a confident mood that the law appeared to be on our side and that justice would be done.*

*"Today. the softest sentence imaginable was handed down to someone who is evil and an obvious danger to society.*

"He was sentenced to 10 years imprisonment that could reduce to 5 bloody years for good behaviour.

"Fuck our Justice system!!!

"Needless to say we are devastated.

"There will be an appeal against this lenient sentence."

# 151.    (a note from Karl)

*I'm hardly an expert on the law, but this doesn't stack up. According to the Sentencing Guidelines, someone guilty of manslaughter by reason of Diminished Responsibility would have been suffering from a RECOGNISED mental condition that affected their responsibility at the time of the offence.*

*Otherwise they'd be convicted of murder.*

*So the judge is accepting that this murderer had a RECOGNISED mental condition …. For which she must have seen medical or psychiatric evidence.*

*And, although the level of wounds was High, the judge also accepted MEDIUM culpability (I understand they were pushing for low culpability). So although Chalkie had his back turned the level of blame is just medium. Which makes me wonder what, in law, is classed as High culpability. Attacking someone while they're sleeping perhaps?*

*The 'problem' it seems is that he had apparently suffered a stroke a short while before the incident and as a result was "suffering from depression and anxiety." Two appointments were made by his daughter to see a doctor, but he failed to keep either of  them.*

*The defence played on this and convinced the Judge that his responsibility was diminished at the time of the incident. Unfortunately both the Prosecution and the defence psychiatrists agreed that to be the case. Strangely the psychiatrists gave conflicting reports just a few weeks prior, so you see, it doesn't stack up*

*My heart goes out to anyone who's suffering from depression and anxiety (clearly, otherwise I wouldn't have written this book with Danny) but - and this is a HUGE but - even though that may be the reason why he's not thinking with clarity, it's no fucking excuse. Not everyone who suffers from mental disorders goes around killing people in such a brutal fashion.*

*It may even be possible a plea bargain was agreed finish the case that day and that the sentence was previously agreed between all parties. Who knows how these things work?*

# 152.   The Sentencing (by Danny)

I am trying to hold my temper and my views. No wonder people take the law into their own hands. This bastard will be out in five years. Is that all my friend's life is worth? British justice bastards!

The simple truth is the bastard lost his temper and got away with murder. That's it. He's got a light sentence and is laughing all the way to freedom. He found an excuse that would sway the jury and he sips his morning coffee while we mourn.

So sad. So sad and fucking pointless.

# 153.    A note from Karl

*It would seem to me that if someone is claiming Diminished Responsibility through a mental disorder (such as anxiety or depression) then a) medical or psychiatric evidence is required and b) if they've committed a crime that is punishable with imprisonment then they would need 'treatment' in a secure 'hospital' (Section 37 of the Mental Health Act 1983). In which case the sentence would have NO FIXED END DATE.*

*Maybe I'm wrong, who knows? I'm just a layman.*

*But if the court accepts Diminished Responsibility then surely an INDEFINATE hospital order should be the sentence.*

*He wouldn't like it there. That's where the read nutters are. If he wants to claim Diminished Responsibility then let him be banged up with an INDEFINITE Hospital Order with the real loons.*

*Chalkie was a personal friend and a lovely guy, savagely murdered as he went about his day job as a plumber. Yet his killer - who put in a plea of manslaughter by reason of diminished responsibility because HE HAD CHOSEN not to attend appointments with medical professionals and not to take his medication for depression -*

*was given a 10 year sentence, meaning he'll be back out on the streets in five.*

*As I've promised right through the book, I'll spare the details of Chalkie's killing except to say he was attacked from behind with weapons capable of serious harm. Well, clearly. And it was a truly horrendous killing.*

*If those who kill - machete attackers, knife crime etc. - are given light sentences such as this, just because they claim diminished responsibility, our streets will never be safe*

*This man should not be allowed back on our streets*

# 154.   My letter to the Attorney General's Office (by Karl)

*Unduly lenient sentencing*

*Sirs,*

*I read in the (online news) that ***** was sentenced to 10 years imprisonment for the manslaughter of (Chalkie), by 'diminished responsibility'*

*The police described this as a brutal killing, saying that "The injuries inflicted on (Chalkie) were horrifying." There were apparently multiple stab wounds, blunt force trauma to the head and two large knives embedded in his chest.*

*And yet ***** was found guilty of manslaughter, indicating that these acts of violence were 'without malice.'*

*Does the court truly believe that ***** stabbed (Chalkie) several times, hit him over the head with something heavy and left two knives embed in his chest unmaliciously? i.e. he did all this without intending any harm?*

*Surely this was murder, not manslaughter.*

According to the Sentencing Guidelines, someone guilty of manslaughter by reason of diminished responsibility would have been suffering from a RECOGNISED mental condition that affected their responsibility at the time of the offence. Otherwise they'd be convicted of murder.

For the judge to accept that this killer had a RECOGNISED MENTAL CONDITION he/she MUST have seen medical or psychiatric evidence.

I'm just a layman, but from what I understand if someone is claiming Diminished Responsibility through a mental disorder then if they've committed a crime that is normally punishable with imprisonment they would need 'treatment' in a secure 'hospital' (under Section 37 of the Mental Health Act 1983) with NO FIXED END DATE.

An indefinite hospital order would be the sentence.

Either that, or the law must accept that stabbing someone multiple times and leaving two knives embedded in his chest is murder.

If those who kill - machete attackers, knife crime etc. - are given light sentences simply because they 'claim' Diminished Responsibility, they'll be back on the streets in no time to kill again. I could name 100 murderers who've been sent to prison for life (with 18-30 year minimum) for *very similar crimes. My fear here is that, conversely, those in prison for knife attacks etc. will view *****'s sentence, realise they can appeal simply by claiming 'diminished responsibility' and their sentence will be knocked down from murder to manslaughter. The courts will then ignore Section 37 of the Mental Health Act 1983, resulting in them being back out on the streets in a matter of a few short years.*

*Surely this judge has now opened the floodgates, and I have grave concerns for public safety*

*I request the Attorney General's Office review Mr Treadwell's sentencing with a view to sending it to the Court of Appeal.*

*Kind regards*

*Mr K Wiggins*

## 155. Intermittent Explosive Disorder (by Karl)

*Many people suffer from what's known as 'intermittent explosive disorder' which, as the name would suggest, are outbursts of explosive rage that is entirely out of proportion to the situation; i.e. road rage.*

*I'm not talking about saying inappropriate things because you've had an emotional meltdown. That can happen to anyone in a stressful situation. I'm talking about going from zero to 1000mph in a split second …. and staying there!*

*Let's face it, our brains are probably hard-wired for abrupt and unexpected violence; it's part of the fight or flight mechanism. The difference, however, is between 'losing it' and fuming at someone at work or a stranger in the pub to snapping violently and murdering someone.*

*A sudden and unpredictable tsunami of devastating ferocity, triggered by a trivial event, that builds into an explosion in an instant is far too alarming to be allowed out on the streets.*

*A geezer like this isn't right, is he? He needs locking up in a secure unit INDEFINITELY.*

*Otherwise what happened to Chalkie will happen to someone else in five years' time*

# 156. A note by Dave the Boxer

*What is going on with our PATHETIC judicial system I just read that a geezer got nine years for forging a lottery ticket*

*And ***** received 10 years for murdering Chalkie in the course of his work by hammer blows and 30 bloody stab wounds. FFS! Something is SERIOUSLY wrong with Chalkie's murderer's sentence!*

# 157.    Recent Sentences (by Karl)

*I did a little research. It doesn't take long;*

*Jahmel Michael Riley (24) stabbed a 39-year-old man to death in an off license in Dulwich. Sentenced (Aug 2019) to serve a MINIMUM TERM OF 23½ YEARS.*

*Ian Levy (54) stabbed a 51-year-old woman who he was in a relationship with. She was pronounced dead at the scene with various stab injuries. Sentenced (August 2019) to LIFE IMPRISONMENT with a minimum term of 21 years.*

*Denilson Davis (21) of Hemel Hempstead, and a 16-year-old boy from the Southwark area were JAILED FOR LIFE for murdering 23-year-old Joshua Boadu in a knife attack in Bermondsey. (September 2019) Davis was jailed for life with a recommendation he serve a minimum of 21 years. The boy was also sentenced to life imprisonment and will serve a minimum of 15 years.*

*Kamari Gordon (17) was handed a LIFE SENTENCE to serve a minimum of 17 years, for the murder of 18-year-old Aron Warren in December 2018. Sentenced September 2019.*

Gerry Matovu (26) murdered a father with an overdose of the drug GBL, as part of a plot to steal from gay men. Sentenced (September 2019) to LIFE IMPRISONMENT with a recommendation to serve a minimum of 31 years.

His partner Brandon Dunbar (24) was jailed for 18 years.

Scott Clifford (33) sentenced to more than 17 years imprisonment for killing his teenage girlfriend. He will serve A MINIMUM OF 17 YEARS and 165 days in prison.

Sean Obazee (24) sentenced to LIFE IMPRISONMENT to serve a minimum term of 30 years. Braeden Henry (25) sentenced to LIFE IMPRISONMENT to serve a minimum of 31 years. This after being found guilty of murdering 19-year-old Abdul Mayanja

Florent Okende (20) fatally stabbed a man in an Ilford street. Sentenced (July 2019) to 23 YEARS IMPRISONMENT.

Two men jailed following a fatal arson attack resulting in the death of 46-year-old Ms Memunatu Warne. William (Billy) Smith (26) sentenced to LIFE IMPRISONMENT, to serve a minimum on 32 years for murder. Elliott Robinson (22) was sentenced to LIFE

IMPRISONMENT, to serve a minimum of 31 years.

Alfie Smith (41) JAILED FOR 14 YEARS for conspiracy to commit residential burglary, conspiracy to commit non-residential burglary and conspiracy to steal motor vehicles.

Mark Lambie (48) sentenced NINE YEARS IMPRISONMENT for supply of class A drugs (September 2019)

Mohammed Amjad Ali (19) sentenced to 15 YEARS IN JAIL after he was found guilty of ATTEMPTED murder. He stabbed a 36-year-old man seven times in the chest.

Kamari Gordon (17) was handed a LIFE SENTENCE to serve a MINIMUM OF 17 YEARS, for the murder of 18-year-old Aron Warren. He stabbed him twice at his home address.

Harry Rawlings (19) sentenced to 16 YEARS IMPRISONMENT after being found guilty of ATTEMPTED murder.

His accomplice, Jay Reilly (17) was sentenced to 8 years' imprisonment after being found guilty of section 18 GBH.

Peter John Knight (72) JAILED FOR 18 YEARS for sexual offences in the 1980s including rape of a female aged under 16, indecent assault, gross *indecency and attempted rape (September 2019).*

*Abdullahi Mohammed (30) sentenced for rape and attempted rape to TEN YEARS AND TWO MONTHS IMRISONMENT (August 2019)*

*Alexander Philo-Steele (36) JAILED FOR 12 YEARS with an extension period of two years for sexual offences against children.*

*Jonathan Mulangala (22) will serve 32 YEARS for the murder of Abdulrahman Nassor Juma, as well as 18 YEARS FOR ATTEMPTED MURDER*

*William Kydd (54) convicted of the murder of 74-year-old Carole Harrison in her own home. Sentenced to LIFE IMPRISONMENT and will be jailed for a minimum of 30 years.*

*Jalal Uddin (47) sentenced to LIFE IMPRISONMENT, to serve a MINIMUM OF 19 YEARS, for fatally stabbing his wife more than 50 times after she challenged him for gambling away their money*

*Kasim Lewis (32) sentenced to LIFE to serve a MINIMUM OF FORTY YEARS for stabbing Catherine Burke to death after gaining entry to her home. Was already serving a 29 YEAR MINIMUM tariff for the murder of another woman, Iuliana Tudos, which he committed six weeks after killing Catherine. Will not be eligible for parole until he is 72 years old.*

*Kareem Lashley-Weekes (21) sentenced to life imprisonment, with a minimum of 24 years, and a 16-year-old boy was sentenced to life imprisonment, with a minimum of 19 years, for the murder of a teenager in Barking*

*Three people who held a teenage girl against her will and subjected her to a brutal, sustained assault have been sentenced to a total of 25 YEARS IMPRISONMENT*

*Simon Pellett (37) a UK border officer who tried to smuggle firearms and drugs through channel tunnel sent to prison for 23 YEARS.*

*David Baker (55) was also found guilty of three counts of being knowingly concerned in the fraudulent evasion of the prohibition on the importation of goods (cocaine, heroin and firearms). He was sentenced to 20 YEARS.*

*Alex Howard (35) was found guilty of two counts of being knowingly concerned in the fraudulent evasion of the prohibition on the importation of goods (cocaine and heroin). He was sentenced to 10 YEARS*

*Peter Windle JAILED FOR 16 YEARS for axe bank robbery. Another man, 36-year-old Jonathan Copson of no fixed address, was jailed for 13½ YEARS. NOBODY HURT.*

*Muhammed Irfan JAILED FOR 19 YEARS for the systematic sexual abuse and rape of a young girl*

*Mohammed Osman JAILED FOR A TOTAL OF 15 YEARS (9 years for drug supply and 6 years for gun possession)*

*Leon Thompson JAILED FOR 8 YEARS for smashing girlfriend's head through car windscreen.*

*Robert Enescu JAILED FOR 9 YEARS for sex trafficking. September 2019*

*Dylan Harrison (18) and a 17-year-old jailed for violent robbery in homes. Five robberies and two attempted robberies. Harrison was JAILED FOR 12 YEARS while the 17-year-old was sent to a young offenders institute for NINE YEARS and nine months. September 2019*

*Lithuanian national Martynas Okmanas calmly walked in through the front door of the family home in Dovehouse Lane, Solihull, having watched the victim's husband leave on the school run. Suspecting it was a robbery, the 51-year-old threw a Rolex watch towards the intruder – but without uttering a word he opened fire with a handgun as she sat in the living room. One bullet went through her shoulder and another damaged her hand as she tried defending herself. Luckily it's suspected the gun jammed and gave the woman chance to flee to the safety of a neighbour's house while Okmanas ran off to a* waiting black BMW. The woman survived. Okmanas JAILED FOR 28 YEARS.

Olivia Labinjo-Halcrow JAILED FOR "18 YEARS. Guilty of manslaughter after killing her partner in a knife-attack at a block of flats. August 2019

Richard Austin (47) sentenced to LIFE IMPRISONMENT for ATTEMPTED murder of ex-wife. He stabbed her several times. August 2019

(sources Metropolitan Police News http://news.met.police.uk/news/tag/murder http://news.met.police.uk/news/tag/sentencing )

I could go on. All of these cases went to trial in the month or two before Chalkie's killer. All of them horrible bastards who deserve to be banged up for life. Most killers received sentences of life imprisonment, and the most lenient sentence was 18 years. And yet Chalkie's killer received just 10 years.

A bank robber was sentenced to 16 years, although nobody was hurt. Two lads received 9 years and 12 years each for violent robbery. Nobody killed. A  UK border official received 23 years for trying to smuggle firearms and drugs. His partners in crime received 10 years and 20 years respectively. Another man received 9 years for supply of class A drugs. If we look further we find 14 years for conspiracy to commit burglary,

*15 years for attempted murder, 16 years for attempted murder.*

*And yet, I repeat, our friend's killer received just 10 years, and will be out in five*

*So if you think this was an ancillary factor in Danny's depression, then just imagine how Chalkie's wife is feeling. She is distraught!*

# 158. So where did it all go wrong (by Karl)

*Well, I've been thinking about this, and I'm not sure we went about it the right way. The sentence was actually appropriate to the plea.*

*The sentence for 'Manslaughter by reason of diminished responsibility' with a Medium level of responsibility 'starts at' 15 years. That's the starting point, indicating that the judge can go either side of that (10-25 years custody), and in \*\*\*\*\*'s case clearly chose the absolute lowest custodial sentence she could.*

*There are certain imponderables in that he didn't bring a weapon to the scene. He just used whatever was available on impulse. And his actions after the event, were for the most part correct. He went to the pub (although I have to ask myself why, was that somewhere he felt comfortable? Had he been drinking BEFORE he attacked Chalkie?) and made a phone call admitting his crime. Also, as I understand it, he's shown remorse.*

*The question regarding this, of course, is that in order to reduce the sentence the court needs to be satisfied that he is genuinely remorseful.*

The issue is not the leniency of the sentence. It's correct, although frustrating that she chose the absolute lowest end of the scale.

The issue is first of all the degree of responsibility, which to my mind should be High, despite the fact that he claims to have sought help (for mental issues), he hadn't sought help at all. His daughter had sought help, made two appointments which he opted not to keep, plus he hadn't been taking his medication. That was voluntary on his part, which alone should place him in a High level of responsibility (with a starting point of 24 years, and a category range of 15-40 years).

So I think all of us, me included, were guilty of allowing our anger to take over and in a knee-jerk reaction attacked the leniency of the sentence when in actuality the sentence was correct. What we should have focused on is the fact that the court accepted 'Manslaughter by reason of diminished responsibility' so easily. And they agreed to a Medium level of responsibility.

Section 174 of the Criminal Justice Act 2003 imposes a duty on the court to give reasons for, and explain the effect of, the sentence.

***** should have been sentenced for murder (not manslaughter / diminished responsibility), with a High level of responsibility.

*The sentence for murder would in all likelihood be life imprisonment*

# 159. Diminished Responsibility

*For a court to accept Diminished Responsibility there is a four-stage test, of which ALL FOUR elements must be proved:*

1) *Whether the defendant was suffering from an abnormality of mental functioning*
2) *If so, whether it had arisen from a 'recognised' medical condition*
3) *If so, whether it had substantially impaired his ability either to understand the nature of his conduct or to form a rational judgment or to exercise self-control (or any combination)*
4) *If so, whether it provided an explanation for his conduct*

## 160.   By Danny

When I read about a murder, the killer dresses in a nice suit and tie for his court appearance, and is very polite, answering all the questions, coming across meek and mild as if butter wouldn't melt in his mouth.

The judge should look at the crime scene and to what this bastard did then form an opinion!

Of course the prick is going to use every trick in the book to get-out-of-jail-free. I can tell you this; this bastard is pure evil and no amount of therapy will help him.

If it was a moment's rage and he'd thrown a punch in a pub, well, we've all been guilty of that, and I could understand it. But to do this act of pure evil and enjoy the rage! He should be caged for life; no TV, no phone, no luxuries. All the luxuries of life that were taken away from our Chalkie. Life should mean LIFE!

I'm desperate to kill him, but then I suppose that would make me the same as the killer.

Just let him rot in jail

'Revenge is mine,' sayeth the lord

# 161.  I have always danced

I have always danced to make people smile. It's a curse, a fine line of being loved and desperately wanting to be loved. I have never wanted this condition because it comes with a price. Chalkie's death was the final straw. My Mum and Dad gone, my cousins gone and reality of the fear that grips me of losing my mind to fucking anxiety.

The world is a playground and time ruin with you but I was wasting it and laughing along the way and making people happy. That was my calling. So I thought!

I love their smiling faces and it feels good to be loved. I can't make everyone like me, but the devastation hurts like hell. If I have offended anyone in this book, or said something stupid, then please accept my sincere apologies. That was never my intention.

The world is like a fucking minefield. It can blow up in your face if you try too hard

# 162.  Sixty Two

I'm going to bed sixty one and waking up sixty-fucking-two

The years are now moments

The days are fleeting

And tomorrow is the now. Yesterday was a thing of the past and the future is seconds away

The body is wiser, but still foolish. The memory fades, but remembers only youth. Tears are now the norm and parents sleep forever, yet I am so blessed and grateful for all those who have made my life wonderful. My wife, Colette, my children, and also my friends and family, far and near

What a journey!

And still the wheels of life turn. Many friends gone, yet their wonderful faces come to life when I look around the town. So many young and fresh-faced boys and girls who were taken so soon. I am struggling with the terms that life plats out. In fact, I find life itself a struggle. But we're all in the same boat, and we all take it moment by moment, blessed that we're still here to hug each other and spread love. It's these wonderful friends who keep life great. Life is not fair, it takes no prisoners, it's cruel, but I count my blessings and thank everyone for their support.

# 163.   Body Parts

Just got a letter for donation for my body parts, and that woke me up! I wrote back that I might need my body parts in the After Life – well, you never know.

Cheeky bastards!

Saw a line of youngsters lining up to get into a club and thought, "Jesus I used to do that." You couldn't pay me to get in there now. Nice flat screen TV, big arm chair, feet up, now that's what I love. Then, on a sunny day, pull the bike out and hit the road, twenty one again.

Funny how life changes just because you're getting older. Can't imagine dancing with a twenty one-year-old girl now. And the corny chat-up lines, OMG! Can you imagine an old man asking a young girl id she'd like a drink? Just the thought of it!

Sixty two! Wow! Now that's scary, let me tell you. But I still fit into my jeans, and the legs will still take me running. But the belly's trying to get out, and the eyes are dimming. I need binoculars to read a newspaper hahahahahaha.

If you're younger than me reading this, I know you've heard it over and over again, but you look at life and say, "Where the fuck did the 80s go?

And the 90s? I think I must have slept through them. It was only yesterday that my children were born. Colette probably stares at me thinking, "Of all the men I could have had, and I'm stuck with him," lol.

So much time has passed and I didn't even see it coming let alone see it fly by! All the children I knew, now have kids of their own .... And those kids have all got beards!

My goodness, where has it all gone?

And don't get me started on technology phones, flat screens computers, self-driving cars, automotive innovations etc. What's next? I hear flying cars! I have 2000 channels on the TV. I've got a phone I don't know how to work, a computer that's got a mind of it's own, and a brain that is ready to be traded in for a new one.

Who knows, maybe the future might hold out hope

# 164.   Anxiety and weak minds

Anxiety weaves its way into a weak mind. It's a condition that comes on out the blue. It's really strange how one moment you're okay and the next your dying because you found a small lump that triggers alarm bells; "Fucking cancer! I'm dying! I need to see a doctor. Am I losing weight? Where are the scales? I need answers. Am I okay?

The waiting room is filled with quiet faces who don't look at you and you're desperate for your name to be called. The fear grips your whole fucking body, yet staying calm makes anxiety even worse!

"Danny, come this way." The fake smile, the white coats, the equipment that has your results on it just waiting to be plugged in. Then you wait like an expectant father and they leave you in the room forever. And all the while you're thinking its cancer and dreading what's going to come out the doctors mouth. Gentle tap on the door and in walks the devil or an angel

"So what's the problem, Danny?"

"Oh, I have this lump. Where? Under my arm."

"Mmmm, it's an ingrown hair."

To some it's laughable, but to an anxiety suffer it's hell. The condition gives you cancer or diabetes, and that's only the tip of the iceberg!

What is life? What are we all doing running around and trying so hard to be happy? I defy anyone to not be affected and just carry on when grief knocks on your door. And yes it's bloody depressing of course, that's what anxiety feeds on.

I'm not alone. I'm one of many that found the balls to say 'help me' and 'how can I help other?' And slowly hands are going up.

"I suffer too, Danny, I didn't know you were too. There are many that want to talk and cry and scream and are troubled by the world we live in, but through it all I'm lucky because I have friends out there who I know love me. They keep me going. Just a kind word and my day is brilliant! If only for a while because every day I fight the demons! I then see Chalkie's wife close up. The pain of losing Chalkie really breaks you in two, and I can't fix the grief. This comedian can't repair a broken heart. To see this much pain …..

Words are silent

So you see, anxiety whispers at me And words dribble out, not making sense and you hope you have eased the pain. Or have you made things worse? Then the anxiety kicks in again. You shouldn't have said that. And the vicious circle won't let you sleep because worry wants to join in, and then of course then depression.

These are only a few examples of anxiety, and they're not easily understood. The dark side of anxiety is suicidal thoughts. Very common, although often a cry for help. The reason people use suicide is to get your attention. But the people who are silent and keep their cards to their chest are the ones to keep an eye on. The shouters are doubters, the boy who cried wolf syndrome.

Welcome to my world of anxiety. You're welcome to it

# 165.    Calm those seas

I have lifted off my veil of silence
Now friends can finally see
The clown that was before you
I have finally set him free

I danced when pain found me
I cried when I was at home
And laughter filled the hearts of many
But I was still alone

Voices played their part so well
They fed on life's despair
And silence in a crowded head
Hoping someone cared

Alas the nights finds you
Anxiety takes a seat
She whispers in your ear
The bitch won't let me sleep

She keeps her all-night vigil
And kicks doors down in your brain
As hard as you may try
She comes back again and again

After many years of silence
To the many and the few
Here's a secret to beating her
Here's what you can do ?

Make friends with darkness
Don't fight the choppy seas

Stay calm and take a deep breath
And make the ocean freeze

Now wrap yourself in a jacket
This will keep you warm
And listen to soft music
This will help you quail the storm

Don't fight a futile battle
Your anxiety won't let you win
But if you stay calm
You'll find that you can swim

Let music drown the voices
Calm those troubled seas
Find solace in meditation
And finally set your mind free

Maybe keep a journal
Just to see how far you've come
Remember to take life one day at a time
For there's no need for you to run

# 166.   Citalopram

Anxiety is obviously a person-by-person treatment, but as I approach the end of this book the good news is that I'm back from the brink of utter madness and self-destruction, and that's due to the brain and its inner workings

Any tragedy can trigger a response that will take you down a dark passageway, but for those seeking relief and brainrest, see your doctor and ask for CITALOPRAM

It will take a few weeks to stabilize your brain pattern but, trust me, I'm back. I feel great! The negative thoughts have diminished and the tablet keeps those bad thoughts at bay. An amazing drug to help you through your darkest times.

I have never, ever been ashamed to air my dirty laundry in public if I think it can help someone. If I can comfort or help just one person, then I'm happy. Think anything you want of me, but there's one thing I will always try to do, and that's to offer help with this dreaded problem ANXIETY

I'm hoping this book has offered a small insight into my world. There are so many just like me who struggle every day to get out of bed. But there is a lifeline. A fantastic tablet that will really help you

I was on Xanax, and I've tried other stuff, but Citalopram seems to quail the noisy brain patterns and gives me a little rest. It shuts off the motor and allows me to enjoy life without the negatives. But you must stay on them, because just when you think you can come off the tablets, the brain goes MENTAL!

I firmly believe that if there a medication out there that can enhance you and your lifestyle, you should never be afraid of it. Why would you suffer in misery when there is help out there for you? Not everything works for different people and they may have to go through a period of trial and error, but there are many great medications on the market to help folk through the toughest times of their lives

I suffered really bad. I went way too deep when my best mate, Chalkie, was murdered. It's a dark, dark road and with it comes knots in your stomach and a racing brain that won't let you rest. The more the sea comes in, the more you try holding it back. That's anxiety, bad thought rushing in. Calm your sea rather than fighting the waves

There have been times during the writing of this book that have been so bad. The worst anxiety ever. Walls closing in, and I may have to DJ a party, so I've got to try and snap myself out of it. But it grips your soul

Many comedians suffer from depression. Once a drug has been tested on you, the doctor will keep you on it until they see results. I defy anyone not to be affected by death. A gentle man. And we're all supposed to carry on. That's what we have to do

Try telling that to my brain

The doctors find a treatment that works for each person, the brain loves to play and the more attention it gets the darker it becomes. The secret is to keep busy, draw, walk, occupy your brain with pleasure, watch a funny movie. The nights are playtime for the brain. That's when you have stay calm and listen to soft music.

I'm hardly an expert, but I am a survivor

## 167.  Happiness is Inside

I found happiness long ago
But I didn't understand
I had it right in the middle
Of both my two hands

I had laughter by the belly full
Age was for the old
The sun was always shinning
And I never felt the cold

I often missed the sunset
I was too busy with my life
Dated many beautiful girls
Had no time for a wife

Children were other peoples
And tomorrow was far away
I had time by the bucketful
And even threw some of it away

I laid in bed for days on end
The sun even called my name
I wasted time dreaming
The rain said what a shame

The mountains I didn't explore
The seas I never swam
I slept most of the time on my own
And life was a flash in the pan

Then one day it hit me
My friend had passed away

How time went by so quickly
And I still have so much to say

I pulled back those curtains
I opened up the door
I brushed away the cobwebs
And walked along the shore

I left my footprints in the wet sand
Watched the ocean wash them away
I spread my arms far and wide
Gave thanks for one more day

I kissed the sky with my tears
My worries sailed away
God's voice was in my heart
I knew I was going to be okay

I finally found my happiness
My laughter was back as well
And life was for the living
And not a living hell

Kiss me with an open embrace
The future we hold in our hands
For now I take it day by day
I have no future plans

# 168.   Dirty Old Man

Good morning everyone ? It's officially come to point in my life where I am now the title holder of the title Dirty Old Man.

Do tell. I get my morning coffee and of course my elderly discount! My attire is sweat pants black for the slime look and a new white t shirt which adds to the young trendy youthful look. And to top off the look a gold watch. Wow, I look good!

I grab my coffee and in walk two fit young ladies dressed in what can only be described as very tight fitting white leggings and white tops. They're both giggling.

So I see these four young lads to which I pointed out the girls and, of course, their jaws dropped t match my own. Now I wanted to see this play out, so being as discreet as a pervert can be, leering all over the place, I knew my hormones were kicking in. And at this stage I'm sure going to be kicked out

I think the bald head and the belly are a dead giveaway, but I'm still trying to be young. So I hung around. hey were paying for their breakfast and in my younger days I would of course have paid and that would have been my move. They pick up their breakfast and notice me perving, but they see the four lads and decide to sit close to us. The young lads had more hair than me and were dressed trendy, really trendy, and with their boyish charms and trim, thin and smooth faces I think the girls are interested. I'm sure their hormones were splashing in their sacks

So one girl asks if she can open the blinds. One of the lads does it for her, and we all started chatting. Now these girls white leggings and no 'visible panty line' that when she turned around I thought, "I could park by bike in there."

And I thought to myself that I am now officially a Dirty Old Man

Anyway as the conversation gets going one girl says to the lad with black hair, "Is that your DAD?" referring to me

My life flashed before me and I was tempted to run home and find all my photos from the beach days, and lay them all out on the table in front of them. But I'm resigned to the fact that those days are gone and I might as well try and pick up 'chicks' in a nursing home

I decide to leave them, and get up for that one long walk home. I comforted myself by saying, "In my heyday, I would have knocked them both bandy!"

But there is a silver lining? I walk in and I'm married to a better looking lady than either of those young girls, and she's in the kitchen, cutting hair, and I look at her and think, "You'd knock those girls out the ballpark."

Is anybody else getting older? Or is it just me?

# We are but caretakers

The world lays in our hands
And trusted with our care
With life in its abundance
On a planet that we share

Alas we broke our promise
As man fuelled his greed
We took everything
More than man would need

Oil to quench our thirst
Pollution to fill our lungs
War to kill each other
Then the invention of the guns

We kill with exasperation
We lie and we cheat
Cages full of broken hearts
We laugh while we eat meat

The suffering that cries alone
The eyes that no one sees
The forests that are cut down
Those beautiful redwood trees

The reef that lost its colour
The fish can hardly breath
It's the future that worries me
To our children what do we leave ?

There are fields that grow nothing
The harvest has turned to dust
And in God's beautiful garden
A world that was in our trust

Shame and blame and sadness
This world is left to cry
As rivers flow though our hearts
Watching our planet die

Can we join together?
Or is it just too late
Is there no tomorrow
Or are we resigned to our fate?

If God came back to visit
This is what he'll say?
What the hell are you doing
You've thrown it all away

This is how you repay me
You had paradise in your hands
You had free will and destiny
I really trusted man

You were just caretakers
To nurture and to feed
All I see is man killing
Hatred and bloody greed

Animals to bring you comfort
Rain to grow your crops
I even made the sun shine
After the rain had stopped

So ladies and gentlemen
It's time for me to go
I shall leave you with a question
One that you should all know

Do you hate pollution?
Do you love the trees?

Do you spread your arms out
And catch the summer breeze?

Do you love fresh water?
Or drink it from a stream?
Do you love the sunset?
Do you know what I mean?

We are but caretakers
With its plastics and it's shame
For the mess that we are in
On man's shoulders are to blame

# 169.  RIP Caroline Flack

So once again a tragedy and wasted life. Suicide is the silent killer, responsible for countless lives and a dark place that no one understands

Money and fame affects everyone not equipped to deal with life. They hide it well and deal with voices, disappointments, sadness, grief and the pain of life. And the voices; the voices that play out in a cathedral of echoes! Trust me, it strikes at all ages and can consume the strongest of people. And yet I hear people say, "I could have helped."

Well, maybe. But the brain has a self-detonation mechanism built in and no matter what you say or do, once a person is set on pressing that button you cannot stop them.

Of course you will try, of course you will listen, that's what good friends do, but many silent sufferers of depression can't take it anymore

I thought I was strong and suddenly life took me down a dark road. Thank God I had guiding lights who showed me the way. It's still not over; it's one moment and one second a day

So many suffer. I'm no expert, but as I say I'm not the first to contemplate the thought. I'm open, I'm the voice of reason and thank God I'm getting help. We are all in this boat and there will be times the sea will be choppy and you have to calm those seas or you'll drown. But then again, a determined brain will cut the life line and drowned!

You have to leave a light on and help as much as you can without drowning yourself. There are days in all our lives that we need a cuddle, a kiss, or just a bit of comfort from a good friend. That's what makes us human

Some people isolate themselves and live a great life and their brain is conditioned to function normal. However, I'm a garden and my friends are flowers and I water them with a smile, a joke, acting the clown, and trying to be the sunshine that will help us all grow.

Just remember, anyone contemplating suicide or anyone who just need a chat, my door is always open wand there's a cup of coffee for you. You'll be helping me too. You're in my garden and, if I can I'll gladly sprinkle water to help you grow. Love ya.

RIP Caroline Flack

Shadows Behind the Smile by Karl

Love Island host, Caroline Flack, tragically ended her Earthwalk hours after learning her trial for assault would go ahead. I never watched Love Island – I have absolutely no interest in the affairs of children less than half my age – but looking at photographs of her she appears to be a lively, spirited and vivacious woman hiding much darker sides of her psyche behind her energy and, it has to be said, her smile

There is no hint of the turbulence and turmoil boiling away behind her eyes

What a tragedy!

She is, according to the media, the 4th person connected with Love Island – two contestants, one contestant's boyfriend immediately after the funeral, and now Caroline Flack herself – to head out on a path of self-slaughter

The fact that contestants are taking their lives is indicative that the show takes young people with passion, vitality and looks, and places them in situations far beyond their mental and emotional coping ability

But what about Caroline Flack? Well clearly, behind her beautiful smile there was something seriously wrong. She hit her boyfriend with a lamp WHILST HE WAS SLEEPING! To go from zero to 1000mph is a special kind of rage understood by few people. Now who knows whether she just whacked him with a lampshade or hit him with a wood or marble lampstand? I suspect it wasn't marble because I imagine he'd be dead, but by the time the police arrived both were covered in blood. A police officer likened the scene to a horror movie, and Flack reportedly had "deep self-inflicted wounds."

Having shared in the writing of a book on self-harm, I can easily imagine what "deep, self-inflicted wounds" look like, and if you're unable to sew them up before you pass out, you can by in serious trouble.

Apparently, whilst under caution, Caroline told police she would kill herself. It seems she was petrified of her looming court date and couldn't bear the thought of going through it, which, in itself, in indicative of the pressure put on people when placed in situations far beyond their rational and psychological coping capacity; i.e. their lack of appropriate decision-making in stressful situations, because I don't know why she didn't just plead guilty and avoid a public trial altogether.

By all accounts "She was a lovely, lovely person." "When she let you in, you were the luckiest and she taught me to love everyone and forgive everyone. She forgave so easily and loved so hard." "This girl was a force and always said the right thing, always made me feel safe and looked after even during her own shit." (Source, a friend, The Guardian online)

The world could do with more Caroline Flacks

I work in construction management. The risk of suicide for those working in building and construction trades is three times higher than the national average. In fact every single working day in the UK two construction workers take their own lives. Do you want more stats? Over 1400 construction workers committed suicide between 2011 – 2015.

Why is this? I can't be sure. Maybe because of the 'macho' image of construction workers, and that the fact that many workers feel forced to "deal with it," not seeking out the help they need, and so the symptoms get worse. Things are getting better, though, and we're talking more and more about Mental Health Issues.

I don't have stats for the numbers of military veterans who are left homeless or who take their own lives, but if society continues to fail to address the issue of military suicides, it may seem to be the only way out for more and more men and women who once served bravely.

Caroline Flack was beautiful, yet vilified by the media, who have a lot to answer for. Ant

McPartlin was fined £86,000 (four days salary) for driving over the limit and hoped he might be forgiven. But it's all forgotten now and he continues to stare blankly at the ad-lib board whilst Dec is reading from it, only just resisting moving his lips in time to Dec's dialogue. In my opinion a terrible and unprofessional entertainer. Phillip Schofield is supported by his wife who he's cheated on for 27 years, and is described as a legend and a hero for his adultery, yet fails to tell us how he's 'supporting' his wife, as opposed to the other way around. He genuinely thinks it's him who deserves the support for being a cheating scumbag. And meanwhile the world has lost a person who, by all accounts, was a "lovely, lovely person."

Very sad

From Caroline Flack's last 'unpublished' Instagram post

"I've been pressing the snooze button on many stresses in my life - for my whole life."

# 170.    Thoughts

Thoughts take me back. It was 1976 and I'd arrived in Bournemouth from Staines, going on the run because I nicked a car and smashed it up and decided I'd better get out of Dodge. I was 17, dumb and young, and a complete idiot, as most kids of that age are. So I ran away to find paradise, friends and happiness.

I have so many regrets and I honestly tried so hard to change my ways. I truly hope I get forgiven for the many shops that I thought things were free. In Bournemouth, the world was my oyster. Then add girls, sun and many coffee shops that I loved going into to sell 'my' jeans. It was a time I shall cherish and as I say some I truly regret and also. Few girls I have bowed my head in forgiveness that I treated not that decent. I was a slut. I think all the deckchair lads were. We all did our fair share of breaking hearts, and I too didn't come out unscathed. A girl called Christine took a huge chunk out of my ego. And showed me that she too could be a just as bad as me! I won't go into details, but she got me good and proper. They call it karma

I remember meeting Chalkie and Dave the Boxer in La Lupa's. I was working there and in walked my future. The path was set to have these two lovely lads beside me for best part of my life! The Three Amigos!

I swear to God we just laughed so much over the years!

The Leicester lads in Bournemouth really made my life wonderful. But Dave and Chalkie and I really bonded. They both took me under their wing, and I can honestly say if they told me to jump into a fire I would have done it. But as with all the guys, Dave found Lorraine, and at that time spent more time with Lorraine than me and Chalkie. Dave spent his time holding hands and kissing Lorraine. But we still all bonded. I was the loud one, Chalkie was the quiet one and when he laughed he always cried

For those who were not part of Chalkie's world, you would never understand it. He was a combination of Clint Eastwood and coolness. How I wished I could be like Chalkie. We spent many nights at The Outlook nightclub, just sitting in a chair and watching the people! Then we would head off to Ella for coffee and pie. We were always laughing. Chalkie was very deep and never said a bad word about anyone. We'd go to the 81 Club and watch Black Tommy dance. My God, that lad could dance!

The sun added to the great times on the beach! The High Street (Christchurch Road) took us ages to go down because everyone was always stopping Chalkie to talk to him. He was like a celebrity. I swear to God you'd think he was royalty.

I was on the beach one day, right by the pier, and who rides by me with a pair of long legs in red tight shorts and a pony tail, and a beautiful body. Sharon! I think Cherry was with her. "Hi Danny," she said, and ended up dating Chalkie and, of course, marrying him. They were inseparable!

And me? I was trouble. I used to walk through the shops in just shorts and a suntan, all the old ladies giving me a lovely smile

What a great life we all had. I would go down the beach and the regular crowd were always there. Jimmy Hardy, who must have laid every Swedish girl that got caught in his Webb. Every time I close my eyes I can still see all of them.

I know I was trouble, and many didn't like me, but we all grow up after a while. Bournemouth will always be a big part of my life, and I have been blessed to have my lovely Diane, who was like a sister, Christine who made me grow up, Karl Wiggins, and Dave and Chalkie

I'll always remember when Karl and I were working together as waiters at the Palace Court Hotel. We shared a room in the staff quarters.

The laughs we had! We'd be crying with laughter, trying to serve people.

We have lost many loved ones and all we can do is carry on. My heart goes out to my lovely Sharon and, of course, my friend Colette, who also lost Mick

I was hoping we'd all ride off into the sunset, but it didn't happen that way

I think loosing Chalkie made me feel how the fabric of life is so fragile. If it was a heart attack, maybe, just maybe, I could deal with it. But for such a beautiful man to be taken has really taken its toll on me. Such a waste. I feel we were all cheated.

My lovely Sharon, who now obviously feels cheated of a life that was taken so soon

We're all so blessed to have stayed in each other's lives.

It can be so easy to fall into sadness, but we all must carry on. I'm so happy I can still visit Bournemouth. I still think Chalkie's alive. Same as Mum and Dad. Because I'm so far away here in California I think when I fly home they will all be there. It's only when I see that Mum and Dad's house is sold, and I see the graves that reality hits me like a freight train

I'm not equipped to deal with death. I just shut down and pretend it's all a dream. My Mum and Dad and Chalkie are gone and the voices in my head are screaming! It's the pain that no one sees.

A friendly voice helps, but that's all you can do, listen and hold each other as the waves crash over our heads. My therapist says to just listen. And I'm slowly listening. But she says always remember to laugh, because when you stop laughing, you die

I'm trying not to die

The bedroom has become my salvation, and I crawl into bed and I'm in a world back in Bournemouth with my memories keeping me company. I can still see all of us on the beach. Collette's Mick smoking his big cigar, Chalkie and Dave laying out on Deckchair with the smell of Ambre Solaire. Young skinny girls, like peaches on a tree, and we were all in the garden of Eden. I think I picked the orchard clean

So we all carry on. We either crumble or we carry on, and I've decided to carry on and let life do what's out of my control

If I can just tell people I love them. If I can just stay in the moment. We all are in the same boat, and we either sink or swim. Please everyone, SWIM

Just remember, no one gets out this world alive. I will need all of my friends. I felt the love at my birthday party – the Bournemouth reunion - yet nothing is ever promised except uncertainty

I have never known such a close group of friends. After all these years, we still care for each other. It's a remarkable achievement. As the song goes "We are family."

# 171.   Karl's Thoughts

What all of us were really searching for when we set off for a summer season in Bournemouth was each other. Something about Bournemouth in those years was the bringing together of 'our tribe'

Paulo Coelho, the author who wrote that great book 'The Alchemist' said, *"Important encounters are planned by the souls long before the bodies see each other."*

And I kind of like to believe that, although of course I can't prove it.

Mind you, you can't prove it's not true, so .....

You see, our life was so wonderful and so passionate because we lived together, socialised together, worked together and loved together.

We were curious. We went seeking each other. And yes, I know there are people who'll say I'm crazy. But just look at those people. Rag, Tag & Bobtail to a man. I'll tell you about them, shall I? They're victims of a conditioning in which authority figures such as parents, teachers, the media, religious leaders, politicians and even their mates – especially their mates actually - define what they think. Their cultural values define their beliefs and ultimately the way they perceive themselves, and so when they call me crazy, I take it as quite a compliment

We all spent several years in Bournemouth, and then many of us drifted away – we had our own agenda, we wanted to explore the world - yet a number of couples from those days are still together now, having made a success of their marriages, and in this day and age that takes some doing. Marriage, with its divorce, broken families and tearaway kids has a huge failure rate, yet 40 years later a number of those couples still love each other and have raised well-adjusted, wholesome offspring who are a credit to them.

Tells you something, doesn't it?

## 172. Back to Danny's Thoughts

I'd love to take all the readers of this book back to Bournemouth. I'd show you the toilets where I slept on the side of the pier, the Haven Hotel where I worked, also Harbour Heights where I set fire to the lace curtains trying to use brandy cooking at the table, the Palace Court Karl and I worked, La Lupa Pizza, the Outlook where I also worked, Stafford Road where I had a bedsit, the Cardinale, Maison Royal, the 81 Club, and the whole beach where I spent many sunny days chatting up.

It was a place where love was attainable and youth was a constant reminder of how lucky we all were. The sun just added paradise for this Gypsy bad boy

I do have regrets. I'm totally ashamed of some of the things I did, but it was survival and I survived.

I shall be home soon

# 173.   And after all that

And after all that, all I learned was to stop holding on to what hurts and to make room for what feels good. Hold your head up. Hold your head up. Hold your head up. Make them wonder what you're smiling at.

It's okay to not be okay

I found out a lot about myself, although it did take time. It was about growing up, but still being young at heart. That moment Chalkie was killed, it killed me too, but I know I have to still carry the torch of life. It nearly went out. Thank God I found myself again. Still holding on

Life truly is a beautiful thing. There's so much to smile about. Stay strong. Make then wonder how you're still smiling

R.I.P. Chalkie

Love ya

Danny

# 174.    A Big Thankyou

A big thankyou to Karl for the love and support and helping me deal with my anxiety! It's not every day you find a good friend who wants to take your thoughts to print and not take the piss or laugh behind your back. He too can see the pain I was in and he jumped in with both feet. It's true Chalkie's death was the final straw that proved life was fleeting and fragile and even strong men can be killed. Chalkie was and still is my hero. If he asked me to do anything, I would.

Now the world just carries on and I'm lost, not knowing what's coming next. I'm dead inside but I know we all carry on. So how does anxiety affect the mind? It's a strange fuzzy, dizzy, out of body experience that frightens the living shit out of you. Your vision is blurred and reality is unreal. It's like spinning really fast then suddenly stopping. Not vertigo, but a foggy feeling of detachment to the world. It leaves you worried and needing to lay down. That's just one of many symptoms that attack the mind. Another is tiredness because you're exhausted

Then there are the crazy thoughts, rambling thoughts bouncing around inside your head. Then as soon as they appear, they're gone. Then BANG, they're back with palpitations and worry!

Once you know what's going on you're able to deal with it. Hence this book. The conditions that help you understand the symptoms. You're going to be okay. Anxiety is only a condition. It's not, and I repeat NOT going to kill you. You just need to recognize the power of the mind and the way to deal with your feelings. Walk, talk, exercise and most of all cry. You need to cry and let out your emotions. It's okay. You'll feel wonderful to release your heart to a friend who wants to help. I found Karl, who has seen first-hand what anxiety can do if it's left unchecked. Karl's written several books and his writing will keep you transfixed – especially his book 'Searching for your Tribe: Wrong Planet People.'

I truly hope this book helps someone who is desperate for answers. There's no easy answers to why the brain wants to play. I just want to close and say a big thankyou to Karl, and I do hope the reader will come away from the book knowing that anxiety can be treated

Love ya, Karl, and thanks

# PART THREE

A few little extras from Danny and Karl

# 175.  Strip Club (by Danny)

She's got an angel-cake body
Not skinny like a rake
Creamy skin
And built like a cake

Rump and round
Firm and cute
You should see her
In her birthday suit.

Big round breasts
Ready to pop
More than a handful
With cherries on top.

Cadillac rear
Gets soapy and wet
Makes grown men cry
Makes big boys sweat.

And when she smiles
She licks her lips
Walks on stage
Shaking her hips.

She likes to dance
At your request
Tells you to watch her
As she rubs her breasts.

She caresses your back
Then strokes your head

Whispers in your ear
Are you coming to bed?

Throw caution to the wind
Quick as a flash
Out through the doors
In one mad dash.

"Where are you going?"
Shouts Sexy Sue.
I'm going home
The wife's cooking a stew.

You may be sexy
You may be hot
But I'll tell you something
You haven't got.

Your heart don't hear me
Late at night
When my lady
Holds me tight.

Your breasts are fake
My wife's are real
And this old man's heart
You cannot steal.

For when I cry
She bathes my head
She's sexier now
Than when we met.

No one else
Could take her place
She's my girl
With the beautiful face.

And time I'm sure
Will take its toll
Me and the missus
Will both grow old.

But there's one thing
That you should know
My wife's my life
My heart, my soul.

# 176.   Black Jack (by Danny)

Black Jack was a farmer
Who hated my brother Mike
In fact he hated Gypsies
Said they were all alike.

The Travellers ran their horses
Up and down Jack's field
Jack shouts back to the Travs
'One of you'll be killed.'

Now Tom the eldest Traveller
Tried to keep things calm
'Keep away from Jack
Keep off Jack's farm.'

But brother Mike
Out of spite
Did buy a bottle of gas
And late at night
Out of site
There was a mighty crash.

Running across the farmer's field
Mike lit up the night
There ensued a battle
That ended in a terrible fight.

Jack had been waiting
He knew Mike wouldn't rest
So Jack pulled out his shotgun
And shot Mike in the chest.

Travellers came from miles around

To say goodbye to Mike
They knew there would be trouble
They knew there'd be a fight

For Jack had ten brothers
Mean as mean could be
And Tom the leader of the Travs
Said 'Leave it all to me.'

Now when you poke a hornet's nest
You better keep out the way
But Jacks brothers didn't listen
To what Big Tom had to say.

'Two wrongs don't make a right'
Says Tom to Farmer jack
But Mike's family were very angry
They had to hold his brothers back.

The night got very quiet
Thought the meeting went quite well
But that was just the beginning
That night turned into hell.

The Travellers watched Jack's brothers
Hiding one by one
Each had knives
Some even had guns.

When Tom heard of the treachery
After all that he had said
'This night shall end in misery
For those brothers shall all be dead

Pass me down my father's gun'
As Tom went out the door
He let out such a scream

The mightiest of roars

'Now you have woken the lions'
As the Travellers call went out
And all across the campsite
You could hear the Travellers shout.

Jack's brothers came out fighting
Each one lost their life
They didn't heed the warnings
Of Big Tom's sound advice.

This is only a story
I trust you read it well
For if you cross a Gypsy
You shall have a taste of Hell

## 177.   Gypsy Warriors (by Danny)

Born with the strength of a lion
Caged with power and might
Carried the world on his shoulders
Got paid to go out and fight

Trained in the hills of Kosovo
Fought in the towns and cities
War broke out in Bosnia
Their names were the GHRIIXIS

They fought where there was trouble
Got backed by powers that be
Sacrificed their lives for others
Trying to set them free

Said goodbye to their family
Flew out on the very next plane
Had a briefing in a secret location
Many men changed their names

They lived in the shadow of nightmares
They went where the brave dare not go
Their lives were such a mystery
Even their wives did not know

Seen fire where there was hell
Tasted blood in the noonday sun
Held hands to help my brother
For we are all but one

Pain became my best friend
Anger held our hand

Rage kept us company
Made us better men

And now we face tomorrow
Our lips shall kiss the sky
And may our God guide us
Today's the day we die

Secrets left in a coded word
A mission that cannot fail
A bible carried inside our hearts
Prevents us going to hell

And while you sleep in trenches deep
Warriors such as these
For life is but a fleeting moment
To fight so you can be free

For the GHRIIXIS

# 178.   Boxer (by Danny)

Only a few see them sweat
No one tastes their blood
The early morning rain
Doing what they love.

The diet and conditioning
Hunger and to train
Takes them to another world
You never hear them complain.

They dance and eat leather
They pray to survive
Distance is the enemy
And time's not on their side.

Their friends they have many
But loneliness fills their heart
For in the ring there's silence
Until they're pulled apart.

Gladiators prepare to die
And dance your duel of death
Later rounds drain your soul
Gasping your last breath.

Tuxedo dressed and cameras
Add glamour to the night
And there laid bare for all to see
The lad who lost the fight.

Once again the sunrise
The morning casts its pain
The voice inside the fighter's head

Makes him fight again.

Never to be defeated
Always reaching for the top
Climbing through those velvet ropes
Not knowing when to stop.

When you shake a fighter's hand
Or a snapshot by his side
Many scars are on his face
But many more inside.

The road to victory is very tough
They try as hard as they can
For every fighter who steps in the ring
Knows the future is in their hands.

# 179. Grief for my Pet (by Danny)

Whiskey Boy was a ball of fluff
Sickest of the pack
Used to cry at night
So I had to rub his back.

Many times he passed away
We didn't know what to do
Took him to the doctors
But he always pulled on through.

He lived a life of luxury
The best food I could buy
He didn't like the thunder
He would run away and hide.

And late at night when it was dark
He'd sneak into my bed
He loved to get under the covers
And I would stroke his fluffy head.

He used to run when he slept
The funniest thing I've ever seen
How I loved that silly dog
Never was he mean.

Always had a smile
Loved his belly rubbed
And in return he would lick your face
And show you tons of love.

But time took its toll on Whiskey
His legs began to fail
We found him one morning
Crying in the hall.

We made a set of rolling wheels
To help him get around
He would run in the garden
Nothing held him down.

But cancer came to visit
Took Whiskey Boy by surprise
I laid beside my best friend
I could see the pain in Whiskey's eyes.

He laid his head in my lap
I prayed we would never part
The doctor closed his eyes for good
Then listened to his heart

Doctor said 'He can hear you'
As I whispered in his ear
'Go towards the light
There's nothing for you to fear.'

Then I felt at peace
For whiskey's running free
The saddest part of this story is
That I wished he was running with me.

# 180. Tears of a Clown (by Danny)

Dance for me
See how low you can go
Here's two more pounds
Put on another show

The lights glanced my face
As tears began to fall
Memories of my mother
As she walked with me into school

I lost interest in the future
Laughter was my friend
I danced away my childhood
And money I would spend

And so I became a clown
And painted up my face
Joined the runaway circus
And travelled place to place

Met the juggler and the fat twins
Fire blown six feet high
Watched tight rope walkers
Even saw my girlfriend die

She was only twenty-five
The catcher let her go
She fell so hard to the ground
They had to stop the show

So when I wear my makeup

I paint a tear for Sal
She was my everything
For she was my gal

I met her in the dressing room
She was balancing on a stool
I was making her laugh
Acting like a fool

We were a great team
As she walked the silver wire
Every show was different
As the wire got even higher

I said she needs a net
But laughter filled the air
So many times of walking
She didn't really care

Then she added danger
A swing came into the show
She would swing so high
Then she'd simply let go

Muscles was the catcher
Russian born and bred
He would let her spin in the air
Then catch her by her legs

On that fateful night
Sally kissed me on my lips
They wrapped a rope around her
And hoisted her by her hips

Up into the rafters
She waved as she went
Never seen so many people

Packed into a tent

I threw a bucket of water
Juggled balls into the air
Laughter filled the seats
But Sally wasn't there

Silence was deafening
As the announcer called her name
She lit the rope in the air
I could see the glow of the flame

Muscles was supposed to hold her
But Sally suddenly slipped
He reached out to grab her
But sadly lost his grip

There she lay peacefully
My makeup still on her face
The crowd went deathly silent
As I held a warm embrace

I still wear this tear
As a memory of my love
She was my angel
Who fell from the wire above

## 181. Masters Voice from the Grave (by Danny)

Sorry I had to leave you
You were my very best friend
You stayed right beside me
Until the bitter end

We went everywhere together
At night you slept in my bed
I always had you beside me
As I stroked your tired head

Your bowl was never empty
Love was always at hand
I remember as a baby
You loved to dig in the sand

You chased your tail for ages
Made everybody laugh
Chased squirrels in the garden
Those days went by so fast

I just want to tell you
No greater love than you
When my head was in my hands
You knew just what to do

You came and laid beside me
And took my pain away
My God, I'm going to miss you
But time won't let me stay

Let me hold you one more time
Let me cry awhile

Thank you for your devotion
You always made me smile

Everyone came to church today
They came to say goodbye
I shed a tear for all of them
But you're the one that made me cry

Don't whimper on my grave Sweetheart
I'm not that far away
I will be in your dreams
When we used to play

I shall wait by Heaven's gate
Until you run to me
You're not just a dog, my love
You're my family

# 182. Brunette (by Karl)

*Brunette is the land surface of the world*
*Terra firma*
*Old sod*
*Dust*

*It is a bag-lady*
*A hard road freak*
*A dock rat*

*It is beggar's velvet*
*Slut's wool*
*Ghost turds*

*Brunette is a leather-lunged shaker*

# 183. Huckleberry Blue (by Karl)

*Huckleberry Blue is the colour of the wild yonder
A harum-scarum hog-crazy colour
A free-wheeling free-spirited loose cannon of a colour
A colour for shooting the moon.*

*Huckleberry Blue is a funky, freaky, kooky, beatnik colour
A radical dude of a colour if ever there was one.*

*Huckleberry Blue is a colour that is not wrapped real tight.*

*It is the colour of old October and pipe smoke
The squaw-candy colour of Alaskan salmon.*

*Huckleberry Blue is moonshine*

*Huckleberry Blue is bleached ebony*

*Huckleberry Blue is mud on your shoes and a laugh in your voice
Taking young virgins into the fields
To set an example in fertility for nature.
This is Huckleberry Blue.*

## 184. Conmen of London (by Danny)

'Two for a penny, Madam
Easy as you go
Come on, give us smile
Take it nice and slow'

That's the sound you often heard
Walking through London Town
Bow Bells rang every hour
Made you feel so proud

Minnie was a barrow-boy
Got his name 'cos he was small
He stood on a wooden crate
Made himself look tall

Apples was his bread 'n' butter
But he tea-leafed on the side
He could sneak into a warehouse
Due to his very small size

Everyone knew Minnie
But don't be fooled by his height
He once hit a fella with a right hook
God, could that boy fight!

The streets of London echoed
The smell filled the night
On the black market dockers sold
Anything in sight

Crime and time the price paid
Gangs fed the news
Death became a quiet game
If you snooze, you loose

Babe was a hooker
She worked Soho late at night
Punters paid her twenty quid
For anything you like

There are geezers and there's bouncers
There are boxers and there's thieves
There are wide boys and there's cowards
Carry knives up their sleeves

Conmen and mirrors play their part
A camera with no lens
'Take your picture mister
Only fifty pence'

Stockings sold with just one leg
The factory made a mistake
There were punters everywhere
Not knowing they were fake

There were lads called fly-pitchers
Sell perfume from a crate
They would let you smell the real stuff
That was your biggest mistake

A fool is born every hour
The streets will spell their names
Many won't hold their hands up
Some hang their heads in shame

Conned, scammed and had

Just to name a few
Clip joint is the best con
It may be old, but it's new

Here's how the clip joint works
There's a woman at the door
She sells sex on a promise
Just follow her across the floor

The door gets closed behind you
She hits you for a drink
It costs you a fortune
But you don't have time to think

Then she orders another
Tries to raise the bill
All she's drinking is water
Then pretends that she feels ill

She leaves you with expectation
But the bill must be paid
You get two bouncers
And NO you won't get laid

The tab is neatly written
Much higher than you know
When you see the price to be paid
This is what you owe

Don't even think of running
A fool will pay the price
Just give them what you owe them
Don't make them ask you twice

Well that my friend is being clipped
The oldest scam in town
There are doormen who'll take your money

And send you round and round

So this is the story
Of conman under your nose
Your greed will water their garden
Waiting for the rose to grow

THERE'S NO ROSE AND NO GARDEN

## 185.   Paul King (by Danny)

Born in Liverpool
Down by the docks
Worn out shoes
With tattered old socks

My dad passed away
When i was just a lad
Mum gave us everything
Everything she had

But times were tough
Mum got married again
That's when trouble started
Along with the pain

Mum was lonely
She met a coward for a man
He beat me with his anger
This bastard I couldn't stand

I was always in trouble
And had to face my foe
His late-night beatings
How far would the bastard go

I slept with one eye open
I could hear his drunken roar
I pretended to be asleep
When he walked in the door

I was only six-years-old
His slaps were for a man
Never cried so much

I would kill him if I can

His marks left his hand print
The bruises were mine to take
I had to be careful
Not to make any mistakes

Time passed slowly
An age to be on my own
I loved to go to the docks
I hated going home

The docks were always calling me
Solitude was my friend
I liked being alone
I hated the day to end

Facing the monster
My head was always down
Catching the mid-day bus
I often went into town

I watched the parking meter man
He emptied every pole
I found I could do his job
Except his money I stole

I met a wide-eyed girl
And told her of my scam
Little did I know
Her brother was a policeman

I denied everything
As the streets taught me well
She tried to say sorry
But I told her to go to hell

I was taught a lesson
Never trust anyone
I was naive and stupid
I was also very young

As I got older
The years melted away
I learnt to drive stolen cars
And had one away

Flying around the streets at night
Acting like a fool
Got a message from my mum
That I was skipping school

Then one day the monster said
Go down and get my cheque
He grabbed me so hard
And got me by my neck

I went down to the docks
And went to collect his pay
I was handed an envelope
From out of a large tray

My eyes lit up with wonder
To see money galore
The envelope was his wage packet
Then the clerk slowly closed the draw

This was my moment
A moment for me to shine
I was going to steal that money
It was just a matter of time

I got the help of my little mate
He had to wait outside

I told him to keep out of sight
And told him where to hide

Weeks passed and time at last
I went to get the stash
I knew the money was in the office
And all of it was cash

Lunchtime was the clerk's hour
He left to take his break
Let me tell you something
This was his biggest mistake

I climbed up the drain pipe
Like a sewer-rat on speed
The clerk left the window open
That's just the luck I need

I broke into the cabinets
He even left a knife
I simply prized open the draw
And another one on my right

I bagged up all the money
And dropped it to my mate
It hit the ground real loud
He didn't hesitate

The money burst from the bag
Coins went everywhere
My mate came out from his hiding place
He didn't really care

He collected up the money
As I walked out the door
I carried another bag
Then ended up on the floor

I was knocked out
Men stood looking at my face
I knew i had to run
So i got out of that place

I knew I had to leave town
I knew my mate got caught
I can just see it now
Me standing in Crown Court

So I went to my mate's house
His sister needs to know
We both robbed the pay office
And it's time for me to go

I rang the doorbell
And pleasantly to my surprise
She led me to the bedroom
I couldn't believe my eyes

There was my little mate
With money all over the bed
I told him I got knocked out
The spring door hit my head

We split up the money
Three grand to be exact
The dockers can keep the other bag
Cause I ain't going back

I became a gangster that day
This is how I roll
Always money in my pocket
I still got a long way to go

Love ya, gangster

# 186. Toby and Tony (by Danny)

Toby was a black lab
Present for a child
All the while a puppy
Made the princess smile.

As Toby got bigger
Princess left him alone
Shut out in the garden
Locked out from his home.

The nights were very lonely
Toby cried himself to sleep
Scraps were thrown into a bowl
That's all he had to eat.

They placed a chain around his neck
To stop him running away
He laid down in the corner
And that's where Toby stayed.

Winter came with sleet and snow
No one really cared
And music played on Christmas Day
All the families were there.

Toby heard the door open
Excited by the sound
He tried to walk into the home
Got kicked onto the ground.

Toby awoke one morning
And walked over to the gate
A little hand was seen
Sliding food upon a plate.

Toby made a little friend
Tony was his name
Tony lived across the fields
Just by Clock House Lane.

Toby waited every day
For Tony to walk on by
They sat away the hours
Until Tony said goodbye.

Early one morning
Tony removed Toby's chain
He sneaked old Toby out the gate
Never to be seen again

# 187. The Dancing Gypsy Boy
## (by Danny)

Once upon a time
In a land far away
Lived a little Gypsy boy
With nothing much to say.

He had a funny-looking hat
And a silly-looking cane
And he danced in the moonlight
And even when it rained.

Everybody came to see
The boy who danced so well
Some say he's from Heaven
Some say he's from Hell.

People laid their money down
At the little boy's feet
He'd give you a smile
Then dance on up the street.

Shouts from the town crier
The boy has come to town
All the bells were ringing
As the crowd gathered around.

He danced for many hours
No one knew his name
Nor did anyone know
From whence he came.

As the boy was dancing
A young girl did he spy

He pulled her to her feet
She was rather shy.

They danced the night together
Tambourine did she play
Her name was Gypsy Rose Lee
And they danced the night away.

Shadows dance upon the walls
To this very day
This was after many years
Since the little boy went away.

So if you see a shadow
And it dances at your feet
Join the little Gypsy boy
And dance on up the street.

Enjoy life and dance.

# 188.   Paprika (by Karl)

*Paprika is an ancient soul with no confusion
about life.*

*It is the colour of the setting sun
Shining right into a cave
Red dust floating in the air.*

*Paprika is the first wind of morning
Soaring far beyond grasp
Lightly touching Nepal
(Which is the colour given to special times spent
with old friends).*

*You know those .....
Drifting kinds of thoughts?
Well, they're Paprika.*

*Paprika is a distant voice that only you can hear*

# 189.   Ochre (by Karl)

*The colour Ochre is a spirit of the past that will
not be denied
It is sunlight walking across the back-porch floor
And it is warm, red mornings.*

*Ochre is the colour of ancient myths
Hearing voices echoing from the past*

*You can smell the colour Ochre
It smells of ripe olives and warm, dry air.*

*Ochre is a small flame
Barely fluttering on a windless night*

*Ochre is dolphins leaping at sunrise
Moving north along the coast of Africa*

*Ochre is a redwing blackbird
Sitting on a fence
And it is the wild, magnificent animal that is you
Watching the rain and remembering
Old winds you have been riding forever.*

# 190. Diamond Diggers of Africa (by Danny)

On sweat backs of mining kids
On blood-soaked hands of pain
They work like slaves in the pouring rain
And no, they daren't complain

We in the west we live the best
Our lives reap the rewards
On broken backs they carry sacks
And mighty is our sword

Diamond drenched with sorrow
Sullen eyes of tears
Father's carry their future
Many who live in fear

A tide of mud to dig through
A spoil for a small price
A cup of water to quench their thirst
For hunger a bowl of rice

Gaze upon your wedding day
A ring that cost a life
Count your blessings every day
For a child's sacrifice

I shall leave you all to ponder
A thought to cross your mind
To see children scratching for a living
And working in a mine

Before you break your bread tonight
Let me ask you one more thing

Take a moment's silence
For the children who found your ring

# 191.  The Miner (by Karl)

I'll tell a tale about a miner
Digging coal for ocean liners
And trains that steam across the land
And machines that place baked beans in cans.

He started work while six years old
Deep underground in damp and cold
No school for him I'm sad to say
He had to work twelve hours a day.

Down the shaft he was lowered in a basket
Although many came up in a wooden casket
For once that cage started to fall
He knew there was no going back at all.

In total darkness for half a minute
Imagine how you'd feel if you were in it
Nothing to see but plenty to hear
As cables unwind close to your ear.

Falling at thirty metres a second
Cold wind rushes up and fear beckons
And change in air pressure does its worst
To eardrums almost ready to burst.
You reduce the pain by pinching your nose
And blowing hard right down to your toes.

But soon your basket hits rock bottom
Too late now if you've forgotten
The items you'll need for your working day
Let's list them quick without delay.

Although a child, he's not so cute

469

Our miner's wearing his father's boots
They're made of leather but full of holes
And cardboard toughens up the soles.

To make sure he doesn't get too cranky
He carries with him a dampened hankie
You're no doubt wondering what good that does
It stops him breathing in the dust.

He's got a tin with his sandwich in
And he's ready now for his day to begin
On the brim of his hat he fastens a candle
At six years of age his life is a scandal.

For he'll not see daylight for twelve long hours
And fetid, stale air his lungs will devour
A file mile walk below ground to work
If your morning bus is late you go berserk.

But that was then and this is now
Our young lad makes the coalface somehow
He may have to dodge a pit pony or two
That'll bowl him over and kick like Kung Fu.

Under the sea these tunnels stretch
It's a tough old life for this little wretch
But if this long journey he survives
Let's see what he does when he arrives.

At six years of age life's not so dapper
For the job for him is that of trapper.

Yet if you're thinking that its rats he traps
To add flavour and body to a stew of scraps
For tucking into later with a glass of champagne
You're on the right track but the wrong train.

'Cause as wagons pass on underground rails
There's quite a danger they'll be derailed
So our trapper's job is to sit and wait
And open and close the trapdoor gates
That prevent them careering out of control
And adding more carnage to this dark hellhole.

By the age of seven he's more mature
And a tougher life this lad can endure
No slacking now you understand
As he loads the wagons of coal by hand.

A year later there's no room for error
As he changes jobs to that of bearer
Bearing heavy bags on strong young shoulders
Sane thoughts drift away and lunacy smoulders.

He spends a final year pulling and pushing the
dragon
Which is what in those days they termed the
wagon
And as he strains against a dragon full of
boulders
The ropes cut painful strips from toughened
shoulders.

And by the time he's ten, his apprenticeship
served
He's spent four long years dodging the pervs.
Which is something about which nobody talked
Yet these boys down the pits were often stalked.

But such is life, and we'll move forward now
Twenty odd years if you'll allow
To find our miner lying on his side
Digging the coal that the face provides.

It's sandwiched between layers of fruitless rock
And while digging it out he takes many hard
knocks
If you listened close you'd hear him blaspheme
As with pick and hammer he attacks the seam.

His other tools are wedges and chisels
And a home-made clock as his candle fizzles
For it takes an hour for a candle to burn
So the passing of time he easily discerns.

But while trying to earn his family a crust
Nothing prevents him breathing the dust.
The air is thick and this man is young
And the disease he catches is known as black
lung.

He coughs and the phlegm he spits up is black
Hitting the rock with a mucous splash-back
Which spreads the illness, though he's not to
know
For with airborne disease there's nothing to
show.

A friend comes along in the form of canary
Which when it stops singing our miner's wary
For deadly gases lurk in the air
With poisonous choke-damp he hasn't a prayer.

The build-up of gases can often explode
Causing roof props to fall and waters to flow
So while dust and gas are the saboteur
There are many ways for death to occur

When his shift is over, he needs a wash
But the bathroom at home isn't so posh
The bath is tin and the water freezing

*His wife's grown used to his laboured wheezing.*

*She takes pan off the fire and approaches the tub*
*Starting with his back she begins to scrub*
*Our miner is extremely tired and dusty*
*But she is strong and notably busty.*

*So while his wife washes his bits*
*He's sure to reach up and grab her tits*
*On the remainder of this scene we'll close the curtain*
*But he sleeps well tonight, that much is certain.*

# 192.    Is the Pain worth it (by Danny)

Good morning world and all who reside in it

Found myself watching a heart-wrenching videos of man's best friend. Dogs come in all shapes and sizes, and each clip showed the love and warm embrace that a dog shows to the, dare I say it, owner. It's a warm embrace that can only be tear-jerking and unconditional love. The dog just wants love, water and food. In that order

Now here's where I'm going with this, and I know the answer myself but I've go to write it down to clear my mind. The puppy comes into a home and it soon becomes apparent that it's crawled under your skin and made its way into your heart and, for most part, into your bed. It's little furry face waits for your every move and cries when you're away. Ot loves you so much that studies have shown that a dog will put its life down for you

So here's my heart felt quandry. After 14 years or so, the dog dies and reminders are everywhere in the house. Then the emptiness the loneliness and then the God-awful pain of sadness, grief and despair!

I'm writing this, chewing it over in my mind, in order to decide if a new puppy in our home would be an advantage or are we setting ourselves up for a knowing ending to our little friend?

I'm still living in pain after my Whiskey Boy died and I really don't know if I want to face the reality of that pain again.

As pet lovers, even if it's a fish it's a loss that can't be described. The question is, is the pain worth it? I look through photos and can't bare to look at Whiskey Boys face. It's dreadful, simply dreadful

I know there are cages full of heart ache? Do I go back and take on the pain all over again? I think I'm going to have to

# 193. Puppies are not presents, they're gifts

There he stayed in his cage
A world that watched him die
A blanket was his only friend
And no one heard him cry

Faces passed his broken heart
A prison for a home
And late at night when it got dark
Once again alone

How he longed for freedom
To run and roll in the grass
He was once wanted
But alas it didn't last

He had a garden with no fences
Had a home nice and warm
He knew no difference
Since the day he was born

He was one of many
That Xmas that was a prize
And when the box was open
Such a cute surprise

He snuggled in a big bed
He would play all day long
How the owners loved their puppy
But something went wrong

He grew into a big dog
Got left out in the cold
Excitement turned to anger
He was starting to get old

No water and no loving
No food left in his bowl
Chained out in the garden
He was left all alone

Many years of sadness
It was time for him to go
The bastard got reported
For leaving him in the snow

And there he lies broken
A big dog with sullen eyes
Once he was a puppy
That was a little surprise

Eight days in the shelter
He whined himself to death
A Xmas present that was never opened
Which the owners simply left

Puppies are NOT presents
Puppies are a gift
They're loved without exception
And all they do is give

There are many unopened presents
Just left under the tree
Just remember they turn to BIG dogs
From a small puppy

# 194.  Women

Very hard to figure
But a wonder to the eye
From top to toe a beauty
But they always tend to cry

They take ages in the mirror
Painting up their face
They can dress up in leather
They can dress up in lace

But here's a gentle reminder
When wine is on her lips
Treat her like a lady
Keep your hands above her hips

Compliment her beauty
Teat her lie a queen
Throw flowers at her feet
Don't question where she's been

Open up the car door
Sweep her off her feet
Tell her she's wonderful
Tell her she is sweet

Lay your coat over puddles
Chivalry is not dead
Run her hot bath
Lay petals on her bed

Lay down by the fire
Share candlelight and wine
Play soft music

Then turn down the blinds

When your wedding is over
You may need a little help
For you may wear the trousers
But she will wear the belt

Romance dances out the window
As you scratch your arse at night
She stares across the bedroom
And sees an ugly sight

Toilet seats and toothpaste caps
Drive your woman insane
And bras and knickers
The size won't stay the same

There'll be screams and curses
And she'll slam a door or two
You're sleeping on the couch tonight
What's a man to do?

So here's a little tip
Before you walk down the aisle
If she's the woman for you
You must always make her smile

# 195.   I got Blues (by Danny)

Born in Mississippi
On the back of a pickup truck
Eating fried dandelions for dinner
And we lived on our own luck

Our life wasn't easy
My mamma toiled the fields
She worked in the mid-day sun
And my papa worked the mills

Many times, late at night
We would gather around the fire
Friends would sing gospel songs
There were many from the choir

I was only six years old
And God blessed me with his light
I found Jesus in my heart
And I would dance all night

Then my father sang
I never heard him before
He picked up an old guitar
As we all sat around the floor

He sat back in his rocking chair
He tuned up the old string
I never heard my father's voice
Man, my papa could sing
The Blues

I fell in love with a woman
On a hot summer's day

Then my fine lady left me
Now she's gone away

I got the blues badly
I just cry all the time
How I miss my woman
When she was all mine

I'm lonely as a child can be
I'm bitter as a snake
I treated her so badly
That was my big mistake

Now I got the Blues
Lord it hurts me so bad
She gone and left me
Left this man so sad

My father smiled and tipped his hat
The pain etched in his soul
Now I know what the Blues are
But life had took its toll

He died some years later
So happy to hear him sing
The world knows my father
His name was BB KING

# 196.    I Blew It (by Karl)

*I still don't know how it happened. My son, Kai, is 22 at time of writing, but back when this even occurred he had only just turned six years of age and we were coming back from basketball practice. Now he always loved basketball with a passion. We'd been to see the Dallas Mavericks in the States when we spent Christmas over there a year earlier and had recently taken the opportunity to see the Harlem Globe Trotters on their first visit to these shores for 10 years. We were also regulars at the Thames Valley Tigers home games at Bracknell.*

*I'd managed to get him into the basketball club when he was still only five years old. The age limit was six, but that's only because of the concentration necessary to learn such a game. They gave him a trial and said he was fine. I knew he would be. He used to go to football practice with 'Watford FC in the Community' once a week and had been swimming forever. So concentration wasn't going to be an issue.*

*He later went on to play for West Herts Warriors, his team once coming fourth in the country.*

*But on this Sunday afternoon he was just six and we were driving back from basketball training, and I'll admit to being a little irritable. I was starting a new job the next day - a job that I was* very unsure about - and so naturally had other things on my mind when Kai started speaking. He just started to complain.

I can't remember now exactly what he said, but he was complaining about people always taking the ball from him when he's trying to pass and how they always tackle him but never anybody else, and then it transpired that he was talking about kids playing football at school instead of basketball at the club we'd spent the afternoon at and I was supposed to mind-read this part and automatically know exactly what he was talking about and ….. I blew it!

"What are you talking about? I don't know what you're saying. What are you talking about? Aaaaarrrrggghhhh!"

I never, ever shouted at my boy. That was the very first time.

I slammed the car up onto the pavement halfway around a roundabout. "Kai, you have got to stop this persecution complex. Everybody tackles everybody else. That's the game. Every place we go you're the only one to be tackled, right? Nobody else, just you! Aaarrrrggghhhhhhh! How do I know what you're saying? We've just left a basketball club and you're going on about football! And expecting me to guess what you're on about!"

*By this time my little best mate was looking out the window trying to hide the tears in his eyes.*

*"Look, I'm sorry, but what do you say? What do you say? I don't know what you say half the time. I have to guess."*

*I pulled out into the traffic once more, feeling like shit. I tried to apologise but ended up justifying my outburst and getting mad all over again on the way home.*

*We parked the car and I must have had a face like thunder as we walked up the path. As we took our shoes off in the hall, Kai said his first words since my initial outburst, "Daddy, are you going upstairs or downstairs?"*

*"Why?"*

*"I just want to know."*

*"Why? Don't you want to be in the same room as me?"*

*"Uh huh."*

*And one tiny, ghostly shadow was clawed painfully from my tormented heart.*

*I lay on the sofa, deeply ashamed of myself. Not knowing how to put things right, I simply stared at the ceiling.*

It must have been some while before Kai came down again. I heard him coming so closed my eyes, pretending to be asleep - as if that's going to fool a kid.

And do you know what he did? He just lay on top of me, holding me tight.

I cuddled him back hard, tears rolling down my cheeks, muttering, "I'm sorry, mate, I'm sorry," into his hair.

Where did this little six-year-old learn the maturity that I evidently lacked? Where did he learn to be so forgiving? Not from me obviously, so this magnanimity of spirit must have come from the angels that surely have a soft spot for little kids with cheeky grins.

As I kissed him goodnight later on, I drew from the wisdom of a lifetime's experience to attempt my apology. I was woefully inadequate.

"Er, listen mate, this afternoon when I got mad with you in the car, I want you to know that I was wrong and you were right. I'm always here to listen to you."

"It's alright, Daddy," he said, patting my arm gently, "I forgive you. You're still my best mate." And with that simple gesture, Kai wiped the slate clean for me.

How did we get so lucky?

# 197.   How to Really Love a Little Boy (by Karl)

*Be his mate. Eat cottage cheese together with no hands. Pick wild berries together. Shiver with him at a football match. Walk with him into the woods so that he can hear the night animals. Listen to the sound of the ocean in a conch shell. Create wonder. Soak up some extra memories together. Simply be there for him. Teach him a sense of his own space. Listen to the voices of the January wind together. Forgive him. Forgive yourself. Take a peddle-boat out to sea and challenge him to swim ashore. Buy him his first diary. Show him the tree you climbed as a child. Eat hot-dogs at the beach in the winter. Play hide-and-seek at the swimming pool. Buy him his first kiddy thesaurus. Always have an out-of-reach cabinet. Take him camping for the first time. Learn from him. Watch him holding a puppy. It will fill you with awe. Climb rocks with him, teaching him about risk assessment. Let him write his name on the wall before you paper. Create secret signals that only the pair of you knows. Collect pine cones for no other reason than to collect pine cones. Wear matching boxers. Learn when to say no. Learn when to say yes. And say yes more often. Never, never, never miss watching him play football, cricket or basketball. Wrestle in a pile of wet leaves. Sit and watch those high, grey November clouds together. Let him know he's loved. Really loved. Teach him about rocking chairs; that there are more memories in them than any other piece of furniture. On holiday, check out a foreign grocery store together. Teach him about sunken treasure. Make choosing a Christmas tree together a family tradition. Realise just how healing he can be when times are tough. Teach him that practice, determination and giving his best will always make a difference. Allow him to dance with a street busker. Read quietly together every night. When unsure, believe him. Have breakfast by the window on the morning of his first snowfall. Shed a little tear to yourself upon hearing he packed your family photo for a sleepover. Realise just how lucky you really are. Hold hands at every opportunity. You're never closer to God than when holding the hand of your child.*

# 198. Cuckoo's Nest (by Danny)

Sleepless memories fester
Like words without a song
A melody escapes me
Why does tomorrow take so long?

Whispers down a corridor
Shadows scream in pain
Windows into another world
Watch me go insane

Leather straps to bind me
A mask to hide my smile
Voices echo deep inside
This may take a while

She shakes me with authority
That calms me to the core
I can hear dreams from miles away
Give him a little more

They call it the mean machine
It takes your breath away
Some in here go crazy
It's used on them everyday

I'm on the brink of insanity
But laughter keeps me sane
They wheel me into an operating room
To look inside my brain

Here I sit in the corner
She's dancing in my head
Butterflies and lilies
Was it something that I said

Medication and masturbation
As music fills the air
Dead flies on the windowsill
Is there anybody there

A gentle smile greets me
As Nurse Ratched tucks me in
Big Chief whispers in my ear
I won't let these bastards win

As night comes to greet me
Big Chief said goodbye
Tiptoed with a pillow
And this is how I died

If you read my poem
I really did my best
One flew east, one flew west
And one flew over the cuckoo's nest

# 199. Here's to the Crazy Ones (by Karl)

*"With each flash a great jolt drubbed me till I thought my bones would break and the sap fly out of me like a split plant" Sylvia Plath's account of electroconvulsive therapy in The Bell Jar*

*Ken Kesey, who many would say was the link between the Beat Movement of the 1950's and the Hippie counter-culture of the 1960's, author of One Flew Over the Cuckoo's Nest, based the book on his trip to an Oregon mental institute. Therefore, the movie, released 13 years later, is based on a real institute and real behaviours of nurses. It can be credited with changing psychiatry by quickening the departure of ECT from mainstream mental health care.*

*In 1964 Kesey purchased a 1939 International Harvester school bus to carry his Merry Pranksters across the United States, with Neal Cassady, veteran of several road trips with Jack Kerouac, as the main driver.*

*They were attempting to a) experience roadway America while high on acid and b) demonstrate that it was possible to be different without being a threat to anybody. The idea was to create art out of everyday life and turn their trip into some kind of a road movie, although this wasn't actually released until 2011. Jack Kerouac and*

Neal Cassady were, of course, the inspiration. The bus, which they nicknamed Further, had bunks, a bathroom, a kitchen with a fridge and oven, a sound system and a seating platform on the roof. It was painted in a variety of psychedelic colours.

The bus's very last journey was a trip to the Woodstock Festival in 1969.

I write quite a bit about Kerouac in my book 'Searching for your Tribe: Wrong Planet People.' He places the crazy ones with rebels, misfits and troublemakers and stirs them all up together until you have round pegs in square holes, which is what our parents attempted to save us from, but what our hearts and souls were roaring for right from the beginning.

"Here's to the crazy ones," said Jack Kerouac.

Karl

# 200.    A Final Note from Karl

*Lie down Danny, let the storm pass over you and breathe the ambitions of your tribe.*

*Do what is right for you. There is nobody else walking in your shoes. Your tribe will walk with you, but no one can walk your road for you.*

*There is a reason behind your Earthwalk, and whatever that is, you are going to have to be yourself to accomplish it. You are going to have to hit the bullseye. And that's what you do best; being YOU. Being a first-class version of YOU.*

*Life is about choices; some cause us anguish or heartache, some please us, some haunt us, while others just hit the spot.*

*Either way, make the fucking choice, mate, and go all the way with it. Do not back off. Go all the damn way!*

*You are one of the forever children. You have the inspiration of a jester, the soul of a backpacker and the heart of a warrior, and you have already done much better than you appreciate. You are supported more than you realise. You are in spitting distance now, mate, just around the corner*

*Not everyone is going to accept you, but the ones who do will never forget you. Come on, admit it, you are not like the others, are you? And that's not just okay, it's fucking beautiful!*

*I believe in you. Flawed, frustrated, cracked and repaired with gold …. but still kickin' ass. I believe in you!*

*Keep up the vibe.*

*People like you really do have the most beautiful souls.*

## 201.   Chovihani (by Karl)

*You can find Chovihani in a thunderstorm, or in the smile of a child, or in the wilderness (I believe that Jesus himself tried that at one stage), or in a rain forest, or a puppy, or a mirror, or by watching nomadic elephants crossing the midnight desert. You can find Chovihani in a legend, or by lying under the stars, or in a daydream, or by believing in magic, or in a conversation with a bag lady, or by dancing around your bones on the edge of extinction….*

*….. or by loving a Gypsy girl.*

*SURROUND YOURSELF WITH HAPPY PEOPLE
WHO ARE BELIEVERS IN MAGIC*

*OR MAGICAL PEOPLE WHO ARE BELIEVERS IN
HAPPY*

*We've covered a lot of ground here, Danny and I, and we've enjoyed every word of it. If you have too (or even if you haven't),* **please go back to Amazon and leave a review on the book.** *Doesn't have to be anything special, just a bit of a blurb, but reviews really are bread & water to struggling scribblers like us.*

**And when you turn the page now - just after the copyright bit - you'll have the opportunity to rate this book and share your thoughts on Facebook and Twitter. If you believe the book is worth sharing, it would be a huge favour to let your friends know about it.**

*Many thanks and God bless*

*Danny and Karl*

*Huge thanks for sticking with us*

*If you enjoyed this book, and I'm well aware that a lot of the topic here is a bit bleak and dispiriting, but if you enjoyed our style of Gonzo Journalism, Danny and I have one more book on Amazon (and I personally have 10 other books)*

**Bournemouth Boys & Boscombe Girls**

**Danny Winter**
**Karl Wiggins**

*In the lead-up to a recent reunion party, many of the old stories came out. We were seasonal workers during the late '70s and early '80s in Bournemouth. Many worked the deckchairs on the beach, some worked hotels, pubs, bars, or nightclubs, either as bar staff or bouncers.*

*We lived off our wits and, yes, from time to time we were rogues, but we had each other's backs and we had some laughs.*

*This book recalls those days and tells the story of bringing a special group of people back together again after almost 40 years. And do you know what, it was as if we hadn't skipped a beat. There were even people who'd missed each other first time around, yet all of us have a very rare and exceptional connection. It's pure magic.*

*Now if you're reading the above and are thinking this was some kind of school reunion with a bunch of old codgers on Zimmer fames, playing inflatable ball games and drinking Dandelion & Burdock, mate, you've got it all wrong!*

*If you've worked holiday towns as a seasonal worker, either in the UK or abroad, then you'll 'get it' or if you're looking to work a season in Spain or Portugal or the South coast of England, then these are the tough but crazy times you can expect. I've always loved wild people and wild places, always been drawn to them, and here are some of the stories.*

*Now, for the first time ever, I think I understand what was so special about those years. Yes, at times they were tough, but we stuck with each other through thick and thin, and especially afterwards when we travelled the globe together.*

*We're not crazy, none of us (well, those in prison and mental asylums might be), but none of us on the 'out' are, but we had lively, buoyant and animated fun. We were carefree at an age when you're supposed to be carefree. The flip side of this, I'm well aware, is that at times it may make some of us feel as if we're outsiders, a lone wolf so to speak. People occasionally talk about us in hushed tones, whispering that we're a bit of a loose cannon. They don't really want to say it to our faces because every now and again we can still be a little unpredictable. But they look at us with a strange curiosity.*

*Some of us, you see, weren't meant to be tamed. We weren't meant to be pacified or subdued. We were meant to run free until we discovered others just as wild to run with. And after all we've been through, we're still standing and we're still laughing out loud. And that bothers some people.*

*Danny and I wish to dedicate this book to all who couldn't be there for our reunion. Some are living abroad, some are in prison, others in mental institutions, and some have passed on. This isn't anything morbid. We just want to remember the laughs they gave us.*

*We're the oddballs, weirdoes, comedians, eccentrics, head cases and hard cases, and Bournemouth Boys & Boscombe Girls is for those who 'get it'*

Printed in Great Britain
by Amazon